done in a day

Jasper

→ The <u>10</u> Premier Hikes!

Where to invest your limited hiking time
to enjoy the greatest scenic reward

by KATHY + CRAIG COPELAND

hiking camping.com

Heading outdoors
eventually leads you within.

The first people on earth were hikers and campers. So today, when we walk the earth and bed down on it, we're living in the most primitive, elemental way known to our species. We're returning to a way of life intrinsic to the human experience. We're shedding the burden of millennia of civilization. We're seeking catharsis. We're inviting enlightenment.

hikingcamping.com publishes unique guidebooks – literate, entertaining, opinionated – that ensure you make the most of your precious time outdoors. Our titles cover some of the world's most spectacular wild lands.

To further support the community of hikers, campers, and cyclists, we created www.hikingcamping.com. Go there to connect with others who share your zeal for wilderness, to plan your next trip, or to stay inspired between trips. Get advice from people returning from your destination, or share tips from your recent adventure. And please send anything you want to post that will assist or amuse the rest of us.

To fully benefit from, and contribute to, the book you're now reading, visit www.hikingcamping.com and follow this path: Guidebooks > Hiking > Canadian Rockies > Done in a Day: Jasper > Field Reports.

nomads@hikingcamping.com **hiking camping**.com

MEMBER 1% FOR THE PLANET.

Businesses donating 1% of their sales to the natural environment

www.onepercentfortheplanet.org

Copyright © 2007
by Craig and Kathy Copeland
First edition, December 2007

**Published in Canada by
hikingcamping.com, inc.
P.O. Box 8563
Canmore, Alberta, T1W 2V3 Canada**
nomads@hikingcamping.com

All photos and original maps by the authors

Maps and production by C.J. Chiarizia
giddyupgraphics@mac.com

Cover and interior design
by www.subplot.com

Printed in China by Asia Pacific Offset

Library and Archives Canada Cataloguing in Publication

Copeland, Kathy, 1959-
    Jasper : the 10 premier hikes / by Kathy & Craig Copeland.
(Done in a day)

Includes index.   ISBN 978-0-9783427-1-5

    1. Hiking—Alberta—Jasper National Park—Guidebooks.
2. Trails—Alberta—Jasper National Park—Guidebooks. 3. Jasper
National Park (Alta.)—Guidebooks. I. Copeland, Craig, 1955- II. Title.
III. Series: Copeland, Kathy, 1959- Done in a day.

GV199.44.C22 J38 2007   796.522097123'32   C2007-902720-2

Contents

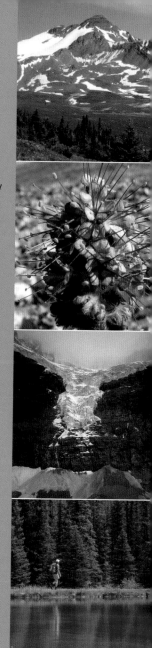

TRIPS AT A GLANCE

Based on the shortest option for each, the trips are listed according to difficulty, starting with the easiest and working up to the most challenging. After the trip name is the round-trip distance, followed by the elevation gain.

1	Beaver, Summit & Jacques lakes	9.6 km (6 mi)	77 m (253 ft)
2	Angel Glacier Cavell Meadows	7.9 km (4.9 mi)	523 m (1716 ft)
3	Celestine Lake Devona Lookout	14 km (8.7 mi)	161 m (528 ft)
4	Opal Hills	8.2 km (5.1 mi)	460 m (1500 ft)
5	Sulphur Skyline	8 km (5 mi)	636 m (2086 ft)
6	Bald Hills	12.6 km (7.8 mi)	610 m (2000 ft)
7	The Whistlers Indian Ridge	10 km (6.2 mi)	585 m (1920 ft)
8	Geraldine Lakes	13 km (8.1 mi)	497 m (1630 ft)
9	Verdant Pass	22.5 km (14 mi)	665 m (2180 ft)
10	Campus Pass	32 km (19.8 mi)	968 m (3175 ft)

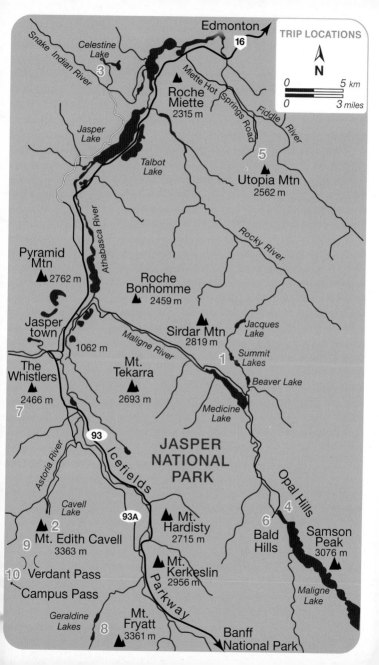

Maligne Lake and Queen Elizabeth Ranges, from Bald Hills (Trip 6)

WOW

Your time is short, but the mountains are endless. So here you go: the ten Jasper-area dayhikes most likely to make you say "Wow!" Plus our boot-tested opinions: why we recommend each trail, what to expect, how to enjoy the optimal experience.

We hope our suggestions compel you to get outdoors more often and stay out longer. Do it to cultivate your wild self. It will give you perspective. Do it because the backcountry teaches simplicity and self-reliance, qualities that make life more fulfilling. Do it to remind yourself why wilderness needs and deserves your protection. A bolder conservation ethic develops naturally in the mountains. And do it to escape the cacophony that muffles the quiet, pure voice within.

Where Exactly?

The town of Jasper is near the top of Alberta's ragged, lower-left edge, in the middle of Jasper National Park.

By car, it's 805 km (500 mi) northeast of Vancouver—a long day's drive via Hwys 1, 5 and 16. It's 370 km (230 mi) west of Edmonton, via Hwy 16. And it's 404 km (251 mi) northwest of Calgary, via Hwy 1 and the Icefields Parkway.

The scenic approach begins on Hwy 1 (the Trans-Canada) in Calgary, where a million people live near the Bow River.

Flight times to Calgary International Airport (YYC) are 80 minutes from Vancouver (YVR), three hours from Los Angeles (LAX), and less than four hours from Chicago (ORD).

A mere 45-minute drive beyond Calgary's city limits, the prairie abruptly ends as you pierce a wall between worlds: the Canadian Rockies.

Within an hour you'll pass Canmore—gritty coal-mining hamlet turned posh resort village. You'll glimpse it, however, only if you tear your gaze from the towering peaks that gird the Bow River Valley.

Beaver Lake and the Queen Elizabeth Ranges (Trip 1)

Just beyond Canmore, enter Banff National Park. To see the entry-fee schedule before arriving, visit www.pc.gc.ca/pn-np/ab/banff, click on "visitor information," then click on "fees."

Fifteen minutes farther, you'll pass the town of Banff. About 45 minutes later you'll pass Lake Louise Village. After detouring to see the actual *Lake* Louise—an astonishing sight that for many *is* the Canadian Rockies—you'll proceed northwest onto the Icefields Parkway (Hwy 93).

The subsequent 230-km (143-mi) drive along the spine of the range—from Lake Louise to your destination—takes less than three hours and ranks among the world's most spectacular motoring experiences.

If you stopped every time you felt the urge to gawk, the trip would take days. But there are four places where you should be fined for negligence if don't get out of your car to take a closer look: Peyto Lake, the Athabasca Glacier (a tongue of the massive Columbia Icefield), Sunwapta Falls, and Athabasca Falls.

About 20 minutes farther, you'll reach latitude 52° 59' 48" N, longitude 118° 03' 34" W, elevation 1062 m (3484 ft). Welcome to Jasper, the little town in the great, big park.

Hike First, Read Later

Because our emphasis here is efficient use of limited time, we don't expect you to read the rest of this introduction.

Not immediately, anyway.

Beyond page 24 it's not necessary, unless you're a novice hiker or tentative in new territory.

We resent guidebooks that begin with a perfunctory *How To Use This Book* section. As if it were required reading. As if books were a strange, new marvel. We assume you feel the same.

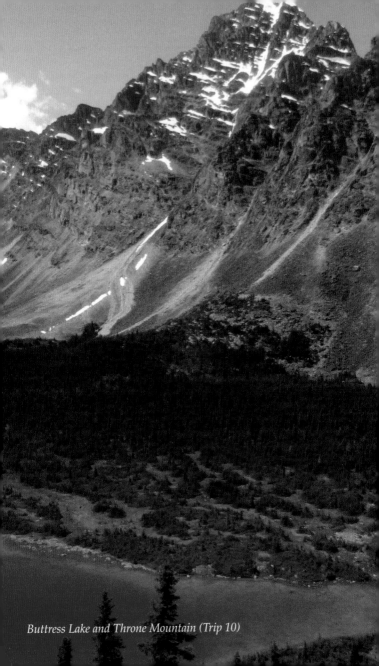

Buttress Lake and Throne Mountain (Trip 10)

If you're seasoned and confident, we figure you'll flip to the ten premier hikes, then dash onto the trail of your choice, just as we would.

Read or hike? No contest. The greatest book of all is the earth itself. Following a trail is a way of turning the pages.

But before Jasper is in your rearview mirror, keep reading. At least through page 24.

It won't take long. And what you learn will top-up your understanding of a place that's going to be on your mind a long, long time after you leave.

The Roaring Rockies

Imagine the earth's topography is a physical manifestation of sound. Hills would be yawns. Bigger mountains would be yells. And the peaks in the Canadian Rockies would be screams, howls, shrieks, screeches and roars.

Other ranges, blunt and cloaked in forest, are shy compared to this brazen northern breed. Here, the mountains are extroverts who bare their full, rock-hard musculature for all to see.

The cliffs are sheer and soaring. The summits sharp and serrated. And there seems no end to their spiky multitude. From a high vantage in Jasper National Park, the horizon resembles a shark's mouth: row upon row of wicked incisors.

These peaks are the guardians of an immense Canadian wilderness. The heart of the range—an area larger than New Jersey—is protected by six contiguous national and provincial parks, where wolves, grizzly bears, elk, caribou, bighorn sheep, mountain goats and their alpine brethren outnumber human residents.

Together, the parks were designated a UNESCO World Heritage Site due to their "outstanding universal value," "superlative natural phenomena," and "exceptional natural beauty and aesthetic importance."

Glaciers tumble down the mountainsides. Untamed rivers careen into the valleys. You could hike into this vastness and be swallowed by it, evading human contact for weeks.

Or you can probe the vastness a day at a time: without being swallowed by it, yet without feeling at day's end that you've left it entirely. Because in the midst of sprawling, feral, Jasper National Park is a unique town of the same name.

The only settlement within the park, Jasper townsite has an unconventional method of governing itself. The towns-people control municipal matters. The federal Department of Canadian Heritage oversees land-use planning and environmental issues. Plus it has a "need to reside" policy: to live there, you must work there.

So Jasper townsite, with a mere 4,700 residents, is and will remain small, humble, reverential toward its hostess: Mother Nature.

Mutating into an urban goiter has never been an option. Jasper is integral to the park rather than an anomaly within it.

The Whistlers above Connaught Drive, Jasper townsite

The town still has the look, the feel, indeed the substance of a frontier outpost.

Yes, there are restaurants, hotels, shops, and everything else travelers need. More than that. There's even a trace of luxury. And what Jasper doesn't have, you won't miss. You'll be grateful it's not there. No glitz. No hype. No buzz.

No multi-story buildings to block your view. No designer-label boutiques to distract your attention. No tourist throngs to raise your blood pressure. Because Jasper has foresworn the "growth at any cost" mentality that afflicts most of North America.

Instead, it has peace, contentment, authenticity, which are deeply endearing to visitors in search of the genuine Canadian Rockies and can be powerfully inspiring to anyone in search of hopeful examples.

In a go-go, grasping, gluttonous world, tiny Jasper is the unassuming Buddhist monk who quietly demonstrates the wisdom of the middle path.

Après l'aventure

No need to endure a caloric deficit when hiking near Jasper. The town has numerous restaurants. Many are good. A few are excellent. Here's where to fuel-up before or after pounding the trail.

For a morning jolt of espresso, an array of fresh bread, croissants, pastries, muffins, cookies and cakes, and hearty sandwiches or veggie pockets to-go, stop at the Bear's Paw Bakery (4 Cedar Avenue, 852-3233), or the Other Paw Bakery (610 Connaught Drive, 852-2253). Both locations open at 6 a.m.

For a vegetarian breakfast or lunch, try Coco's Cafe (608 Patricia Street, 852-4550). They brew specialty coffees (organic and fair trade, of course), concoct fruit smoothies, dish out scrambled tofu, serve veggie burgers, and won't respond with an ignorant stare when you say "I'm a vegan."

The Black Sheep Cafe and Grill (407 Patricia Street, 852-9788) serves comfort food—burritos, burgers, handcut fries—and offers breakfast all day, including omelettes, crepes, scones, bagels, and fruit salad.

For an exceptional dinner, make reservations at Andy's Bistro (606 Patricia Street, 852-4559). Andy asks that you "Allow at least two hours to enjoy your meal, because good food takes time to create, and all our meals are prepared a la minute: to order." You can peruse the current menu at www.andysbistro. com. Andy also offers a wine list that lives up to his dining room's wine-cellar appearance.

At Tekarra Restaurant (1 km / 0.6 mi south of town on Hwy 93A), you can dine in the historic lodge or outside among the pines. Dishes such as snapper in jungle-curry sauce, macadamia-nut lamb, and banana-crusted chicken with mango chutney have earned Tekarra glowing reviews, so dinner reservations (852-4624) are necessary.

The Jasper Park Lodge, though elegant, is sufficiently rustic that it appears to belong here. It was built in 1922 to accom-

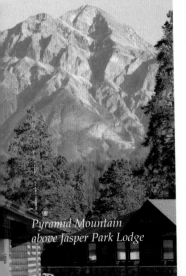

modate wealthy railway passengers. Guests have included Marilyn Monroe and Joe DiMaggio, Sir Arthur Conan Doyle, King George VI and Princess Elizabeth, and Bobby and Ethel Kennedy. The resort comprises log cabins and cedar chalets tucked into the forest near the shore of Lac Beauvert, numerous restaurants, and a platoon of chefs. Visit www.fairmont.com/jasper to marvel at all the dining options. Phone 852-3301 for dinner reservations, or 1-800-257-7544 to book a room.

Pyramid Mountain above Jasper Park Lodge

If you prefer to cook for yourself, but retreating to a private, lakeside cabin appeals to you, consider staying at the Patricia Lake Bungalows. You'll find granite countertops in the epicurean kitchens, and plasma TVs beside the mountain-rock fireplaces. Visit www.patricialakebungalows.com to learn more. Phone 852-3560 or 888-499-6848 for reservations.

Jasper also has a flourishing Home Accommodation Association. More than 100 rooms in private homes are available for rent. All are inspected by Parks Canada, most are a short walk from the town centre, many offer breakfast. They range from spare bedrooms, to apartments with fully-equipped kitchens. Visit www.stayinjasper.com for a list. Or pick one up at the Parks Canada Info Centre (500 Connaught Drive).

Okay. You've gone hiking, established your temporary Jasper residence, and quelled your hunger. If you're wondering "What next?" here are a few answers.

Stop by the Jasper Artists Guild in the old fire hall, on the corner of Patricia and Elm streets. They support local artists by increasing awareness of visual fine arts in the community.

Patricia Street, Jasper townsite

In addition to maintaining the Brush Fire gallery, they arrange exhibits at local cafes, restaurants and businesses. Learn more by visiting www.jasperartistsguild.com or phoning 852-3554.

On a loop walk down Connaught Drive and back along Patricia Street you'll see nearly every shop in town, so it's possible to assess each one for yourself. Recommendations? Check out…

The Tea Leaf Boutique (626 Connaught, 852-5552) for lively women's fashions (dresses, handbags, footwear, jewelry), extraordinary loose-leaf teas, and distinctive teapots, infusers and travel mugs.

Jasper Rock and Jade (620a Connaught, 852-3631) for intriguing fossils, salubrious crystals, beautiful stones, fine pottery, and eclectic rock jewelry. Take special note of the ammolite: mineralized shells of squid-like creatures. It's traditional for Alberta's public officials to present visiting dignitaries with ammolite jewelry.

But if it's a hot, sunny day, and you're not hiking, you can do better than go shopping. You can go to heaven.

From the junction with Connaught Drive at the north end of Jasper townsite, drive Hwy 16 north 1.8 km (1.1 mi). Turn right (east) onto Maligne Lake Road (signed for Jasper Park Lodge), cross the Athabasca River bridge, go right (south), then take the first left.

You'll soon pass the west shore of Lake Annette and quickly reach the south shore of Lake Edith. Both bodies of water afford blissful swimming. Shallow enough that they warm quickly and thoroughly each summer, you'll likely find you can stay in as long as you want.

Most Canadian Rocky Mountain lakes are frigid. If you plunge in, your nerve endings will launch you back out—shrieking—even before your brain receives the message: "Mother of God, this cold!" Only a polar bear could actually *swim* in them.

Pyramid Mountain above Lake Edith

By comparison, Edith and Annette are hot tubs. Yet you can admire the surrounding peaks while you're doing the backstroke. Check out the scenery at both lakes, then dive into whichever appeals to you. Bear in mind: Edith is a bit deeper, therefore slightly cooler.

You prefer scalding-hot water? Head to Miette Hot Springs, where the 54° C (130°F) outdoor pool will soothe your trail-weary muscles and joints. You can rent a swimsuit and towel. Lockers are also available. Phone (800) 767-1611 to confirm it's open, then drive Hwy 16 north about 42 km (26 mi) from Jasper townsite. Turn right (southeast) onto Miette Hot Springs Road and follow it 17 km (10.5 mi) to the road's end parking lot.

Though a steamy soak feels more relaxing, a gentle walk the day after a strenuous hike is equally therapeutic. Near Jasper, *the* place to stroll is Maligne Canyon—a fascinating limestone chasm.

The upper canyon—between the first and third bridges—is popular with tourists. That's where the canyon is deepest (55 m / 180 ft) and narrowest (1.8 m / 6 ft), and where the falls are most impressive. But approaching from below—starting at the sixth bridge—is more tranquil and intriguing.

A 4-km (2.5-mi) trail links the sixth and first bridges. Elevation gain: 145 m (476 ft). From near its confluence with the Athabasca Rivers, you'll follow the Maligne River upstream, through a forest of pine, spruce, poplar and birch.

The grade steepens above the fifth bridge, where you reach the canyon. Between the third and first bridges, you'll cross water-polished bedrock and see potholes in the canyon walls.

To reach the trailhead, follow Connaught Drive to the north end of Jasper townsite, then drive Hwy 16 north 1.8 km (1.1 mi). Turn right (east) onto Maligne Lake Road (signed for Jasper Park Lodge), cross the Athabasca River bridge, then go left (north-northeast). At 4.1 km (2.5 mi) turn left (north). Reach the sixth bridge picnic area at 5.7 km (3.5 mi). The trail begins on the far (northeast) side of the bridge spanning the Maligne River. To begin the walk, go right (southeast).

Big and Untamed

Ringed by more than a dozen lakes, near the confluence of the Miette and Athabasca rivers, at the base of the Colin, Maligne, Trident, and Victoria Cross ranges, the town of Jasper is in a serene mountain enclave: the Athabasca River Valley.

A mere 8,000 years ago, a great swath of glacial ice covered most of the valley. The climate warmed, the ice melted, and plants began colonizing the post-glacial basin. Insects, birds and other animals followed. Luxuriant flora and thriving fauna attracted the plains-dwelling aboriginal people.

From just beyond the east edge of the Rockies, native hunters ventured into the Athabasca River Valley tracking deer, elk and bighorn sheep. The remains of campsites indicate human habitation more than 3,000 years ago. No evidence of permanent settlements has been found, however, probably due to the fiercely cold winters and deep snows.

Prior to the arrival of Europeans, the Sarcee tribe frequented both sides of the Rockies north of the Athabasca River. Archaeologists also believe the Shuswap tribe roamed what is now eastern Jasper Park.

Numerous other tribes probed the Rockies as native populations

Maligne Canyon

reached their all-time high. Relations were cordial, trade frequent, conflict minimal. But North American aboriginal culture was shattered in the 1700s, when Europeans trickled then flooded across the continent, introducing guns, horses and new diseases.

Tribal discord increased as dramatic power shifts occurred. Territorial conflicts broke out. Violence proliferated. A small-pox epidemic annihilated 60% of the western aboriginal population. Meanwhile, the white invaders slaughtered the great buffalo herds—a critical Native food source—nearly to extinction.

The first European to approach the Canadian Rockies did so in 1754. Subsequent explorers encountered the "Great River of the Woods," later named the Athabasca River. In the late 1700s and early 1900s, the North West and Hudson's Bay companies expanded their fur trapping-and-trading enterprises here.

Missionaries soon followed, establishing churches throughout the western prairies and eastern Rockies.

The first trading post was established in 1799 at Rocky Mountain House, west of Red Deer. Trading, however, was not the primary function of this and other posts. Instead, they stabled horses and sheltered company employees plying the trail.

English-Canadian explorer David Thompson was the first European to visit the area where Jasper townsite was eventually founded. Known to natives as "Stargazer," he passed through in 1810 on his historic mapping expedition to the Pacific Ocean via Athabasca Pass.

Thompson directed some of his men to stay behind and build a trading post. No trace of it remains, and its precise location is unknown, but it was near the Athabasca River, across from where Jasper townsite is today, perhaps where Jasper Park Lodge now stands. Named "Henry House" (after construction-crew boss William Henry) it was the earliest significant structure built by non-natives in the Canadian Rockies and marked the inception of Jasper townsite.

Jasper Lake where the Athabasca River widens north of town, from Highway 16

After Thompson pioneered the Athabasca trade route, fur traders followed. Each spring and fall, brigades of mainly French-speaking voyageurs (travelers) departed Lake Superior and paddled northwest across the waterways of the Canadian Shield to the North Saskatchewan River. From Edmonton, they portaged to the Athabasca River, which they followed upstream to the Rockies. They then continued on horseback to "la montagne de la gran traverse" (the mountain of the great crossing). Now called *Mt. Edith Cavell*, it's the icy peak southwest of Jasper townsite (see photo on page 41). Just beyond it is the Whirlpool River, which they followed west to Athabasca Pass.

Somewhere between the Athabasca and Columbia rivers, the westbound fur brigade met their counterparts—the eastbound brigade—with whom they exchanged goods for furs. Each brigade then reversed its route. Many voyageur place names endure, lending a colourful ambience to the Jasper area. The prominent mountain northeast of Jasper Lake, for example, is *Roche Miette*.

The name *Jasper*, however, has a prosaic origin. In 1813 the North West Company built a trading post at Brûlé Lake, west of present-day Hinton. Jasper Hawes managed it, so traders called it "Jasper's House" and eventually "Jasper House." In 1829 the company moved the post into the mountains, near the confluence of the Snake Indian and Athabasca rivers, across from Roche Miette.

Jasper House was abandoned in 1884, because the fur trade had declined, but by then the name *Jasper* was synonymous with the entire region. So in 1907, when the Dominion Government protected a vast tract of wilderness surrounding the upper Athabasca River Valley, they named it "Jasper Forest Park."

Visitors began trickling in, but tourism never boomed the way it did in Banff Park, where the railroad arrived in 1883—nearly three decades before track was laid to Jasper townsite.

Jasper Park's first resident superintendent built a stone-and-log home in 1913 that still stands today. It's the town's most distinctive structure—quietly commanding yet warmly inviting—and now serves as the Jasper Information Centre, a purpose for which its frontier style is ideally suited.

About that time, the Pocahontas coal mine opened near the townsite. A small mining community developed, but it dispersed a decade later when the price of coal slumped and the mine closed.

Jasper's first school opened in 1914. A road linking the town with Edmonton was completed in 1928. And in 1930, Jasper Forest Park was renamed *Jasper National Park*.

By 1940 the Icefields Parkway pierced Banff Park's northern reaches near the Columbia Icefield and connected the towns of Banff and Jasper. This and other park infrastructure was largely built during WWI by Slavic Canadian internees, and during the Great Depression through public works projects funded by the Canadian Unemployment and Farm Relief Act.

Marmot Basin Ski Area opened in 1966, significantly boosting winter visitation to Jasper. Tourism further increased in the 1970s when Edmonton (four hours distant by car) grew and prospered along with Alberta's petroleum industry.

Yet Marmot is still known for short lift lines, and its huge, alpine bowls remain uncrowded. Likewise, most of Jasper Park's 100 backcountry campgrounds and 1200 km (660 mi) of hiking trails are always tranquil. And nearby Miette Hot Springs is relaxing not only because the water is hot enough to melt your bones but because it's never mobbed.

The reason for this placid atmosphere is that the most northerly of Canada's Rocky Mountain parks is also the largest and most remote. Jasper Park, comprising 10,878 sq km (4200 sq mi), attracts about 1.9 million visitors each year, while Banff Park, comprising 6641 sq km (2564 sq mi), attracts roughly 3 million.

Due to its sprawling size and wilderness integrity, Jasper Park ranks among the world's great protected ecosystems. Large mammals—elk, bighorn sheep, mountain goats, caribou—roam freely here, which ensures a thriving population of carnivores: bears, mountain lions, wolves and… the elusive bigfoot?

Jasper Park Info Centre

When David Thompson was in the Jasper region, he saw the footprint of a massive animal that he was unable to identify. Here's what he wrote in his journal:

"The sight of the track of that large beast staggered me."

That proves nothing, of course. But Thompson was among the world's most knowledgeable and experienced explorers, so it does give one pause.

Reports of giant apes roaming North American forests have long persisted. The Nuxalk Indians of present-day Bella Coola, B.C., called the creature "boq." Natives on Vancouver Island called it "matlox." The Coast Salish called it "sésqec," which is the closest etymological root of "sasquatch."

Whether or not Jasper has ever been home to the towering bipedal hominoid referred to as *Gigantopithecus blacki* remains a mystery. What is evident to anyone who's thoroughly probed the park's backcountry, however, is that it's sufficiently big and untamed that it *feels* like it could accommodate such a creature.

Given how far humanity has distanced itself from the natural world, that's a very good feeling.

Relaxing at the first Summit Lake (Trip 1)

Sky Jazz

Some mountains, especially volcanoes—Mt. Fuji, Mt. Kilimanjaro, Mt Rainier for example—have what appear from a distance to be relatively smooth slopes. Like the chord progression in a traditional song, they break the horizon gently, rise unbroken to a crescendo, then gradually resolve back into the horizon.

Not so the Canadian Rockies. In musical terms, these mountains are avant-garde. They've abandoned not just chord progressions, but chords, scales, and rhythmic meters in favour of improvisation. The resulting shapes are fantastic. Infinitely varied. Jazz set in stone, lofted into the sky.

There were no mountains here 1.5 billion years ago. This was the north shore of a vast supercontinent surrounded by shallow, warm seas teeming with the earliest forms of multicellular life.

Between 140 million and 45 million years ago, two separate collisions of continental plates (moving slower than the speed of a growing fingernail) pushed up sedimentary rock—limestone, dolomite, shale, sandstone, quartz—from the ancient ocean floor. Thrust skyward, it formed the Canadian Rockies, which are now a middle-aged mountain range.

In Jasper National Park, there are many types of mountains: complex, irregular, anticlinal, synclinal, castellate, dogtooth, and sawback. But the structure most visitors soon think of as "classically Jasper" are called *dip-slope* mountains. One side is steep, the other gradual. The Endless Chain, looming above the northeast side of the Icefields Parkway, about 50 km (31 mi) southeast of Jasper townsite, is a dip-slope massif.

Once built, mountains are immediately torn down. It's slow, tedious work. Glacial ice is the patient, demolition-crew boss. Its erosional influence is evident in the U-shape of the Athabasca River Valley, and in the numerous hanging valleys issuing waterfalls.

Though glaciers the world over are now mere fragments compared to their ice-age magnitude, and their power to erode has diminished, more than 1,000 of them remain in Jasper National Park.

Glacial meltwater also erodes mountains, and there's a lot of it here. The Columbia Icefield, at the park's southern tip, is a hydrological apex. It feeds streams and rivers flowing into the Pacific, Atlantic and Arctic oceans.

Before fully heeding the call of gravity, however, water tends to pool up in lakes, which in Jasper Park can look surprisingly like spilled paint. You'll see every blue-green shade in the Benjamin Moore *Designer Classics* colour palette. That's because the water contains suspended rock particles (ground to dust by glaciers) that reflect sunlight.

All mountains are works in progress. But more than most, the Canadian Rockies have been immortalized in their present state by humankind's favourite art form: film.

Hollywood focused its cameras here before moving pictures had sound. Like a burly stuntman, the range has successfully stood-in for the Swiss Alps many times.

Even the iconic, wild west that's permanently lodged between most Americans' ears is largely composed of imagery filmed in the Canadian Rockies.

Wildlife

The readily visible presence of wildlife is among the chief attractions of visiting the Canadian Rocky Mountain national parks.

Here, it's surprisingly easy to see where you stand in the food chain. Discovering you're several rungs down—by encountering a bear, for example—is both humbling and exhilarating.

It's also a healthy experience, given our species has the arrogant and harmful habit of erroneously thinking of itself as top dog.

Elk beside Talbot Lake

But bears—grizzlies as well as blacks—are just one of many kinds of animals you might observe. Other creatures big and small are more frequently visible.

Watch for bats, owls, eagles (bald and golden), red-tailed hawks, osprey, falcons, jays, woodpeckers, bluebirds, Clark's nutcrackers, ptarmigan, loons, herons, and mallards.

Also be on the lookout for chipmunks, squirrels, weasels, otter, raccoons, skunks, deer, lynx, coyotes, mountain goats, bighorn sheep, caribou, and moose.

Elk frequent Jasper townsite. In the evening, watch for porcupines waddling out of the forest and beavers cruising ponds. On alpine trails, you'll likely see pikas and marmots.

It's a rare and fortunate hiker who glimpses a wolf, wolverine, or cougar.

Bears

Bears are not a problem in the Canadian Rockies. But oblivious hikers often endanger themselves, other people, and the bears.

Knowledge and anticipation are all you need to hike confidently, secure in the understanding that bears pose little danger.

Only a couple hundred grizzly bears roam the Canadian Rocky Mountain national parks. The black-bear population is comparable. You're more likely to see a bear while driving the Icefields Parkway than while hiking most backcountry trails.

Grizzly bear

Grizzlies are the slowest reproducing land animals in North America. Only the musk ox is slower. So Jasper Park's grizzly population will remain small.

The Jasper Information Centre posts trail reports that include bear warnings and closures. Check these before your trip; adjust your plans accordingly.

Grizzlies and blacks can be difficult for an inexperienced observer to tell apart. Both species range in colour from nearly white to cinnamon to black. Full-grown grizzlies are much bigger, but a young grizzly can resemble an adult black bear, so size is not a good indicator.

The most obvious differences? Grizzlies have a dished face; a big, muscular shoulder hump; and long, curved front claws. Blacks have a straight face; no hump; and shorter, less visible front claws.

Grizzlies are potentially more dangerous than black bears, although a black bear sow with cubs can be just as aggressive. Be wary of all bears.

Any bear might attack when surprised. If you're hiking, and forest or brush limits your visibility, you can prevent surprising a bear by making noise. Bears hear about as well as humans. Most are as anxious to avoid an encounter as you are. If you warn them of your presence before they see you, they'll usually clear out.

So use the most effective noisemaker: your voice.

Black bear

Shout loudly. Keep it up. Don't be embarrassed. Be safe. Yell louder near streams, so your voice carries over the competing noise. Sound off more frequently when hiking into the wind. That's when bears are least able to hear or smell you coming.

To learn more, read *Bears & People* at www. pc.gc.ca/pn-np/ab/jasper, or download the *Bears Beware!* MP3 at hikingcamping. com. Go to Guidebooks > Hiking > Canadian Rockies

Bears' strongest sense is smell. They can detect an animal carcass several miles away. So don't take odourous foods on your dayhike, and never leave food scraps in your wake. Otherwise you're teaching bears to think "humans = food," furthering the possibility of a dangerous encounter.

Bears are smart. They quickly learn to associate a particular place, or people in general, with an easy meal. They become habituated and lose their fear of man. A habituated bear is a menace to any hiker within its range.

If you see a bear, don't look it in the eyes; it might think you're challenging it. Never run. Initially be still. If you must move, do it in slow motion. Bears are more likely to attack if you flee, and they're fast. A grizzly can rapidly accelerate to 50 kph (31 mph)—faster than an Olympic gold medalist sprinter. And it's a myth that bears can't run downhill.

They're also strong swimmers. Despite their ungainly appearance, they're excellent climbers too. Nevertheless, climbing a tree can be an option for escaping an aggressive bear. Some people have saved their lives this way. Others have been caught in the process.

To be out of reach of an adult bear, you must climb at least 10 m/yd very quickly, something few people are capable of. It's generally best to avoid provoking an attack by staying calm, initially standing your ground, making soothing sounds to convey a nonthreatening presence, then retreating slowly.

What should you do when a bear charges?

If you're certain it's a lone black bear—not a sow with cubs, not a grizzly—fighting back might be effective.

If it's a grizzly, and contact seems imminent, lie face down, with your legs apart and your hands clasped behind your neck. This is safer than the fetal position, which used to be recommended, because it makes it harder for the bear to flip you over.

If you play dead, a grizzly is likely to break off the attack once it feels you're no longer a threat. Don't move until you're sure the bear has left the area, then slowly, quietly, get up and walk away. Keep moving, but don't run.

Arm yourself with pepper spray as a last defense. Keep it in a holster, on your hip belt or shoulder strap, where you can grab it fast. Many people have successfully used it to turn back charging bears.

Cayenne pepper, highly irritating to a bear's sensitive nose, is the spray's active ingredient. Without causing permanent injury, it disables the bear long enough to let you escape.

But vigilance and noise making should prevent you from ever having to spray. Do so only if you're convinced your life is at risk. You can buy pepper spray at outdoor stores. Counter Assault is a reputable brand.

Remember: your safety is not the only consideration. Bears themselves are at risk when confronted by people. Protecting these magnificent creatures is a responsibility hikers must accept.

Whenever bears act aggressively, they're following their natural instinct for self preservation. Often they're protecting their cubs or a food source. Yet if they maul a hiker, they're likely to be killed, or captured and moved, by wildlife management officers.

Merrily disregarding bears is foolish and unsafe. Worrying about them is miserable and unnecessary. Everyone occasionally feels afraid when venturing deep into the mountains, but knowledge and awareness can quell fear of bears.

Just take the necessary precautions and remain guardedly alert. Experiencing the grandeur of the Canadian Rockies is certainly worth risking the remote possibility of a bear encounter.

Cougars

You'll probably never see a cougar. But they live in the Canadian Rockies, and they can be dangerous, so you should know a bit about them.

Elsewhere referred to as a puma, mountain lion, or panther, the cougar is an enormous, graceful cat. An adult male can reach the size of a big human: 80 kg (175 lb), and 2.4 m (8 ft) long including a 1-m (3-ft) tail. In the Canadian Rockies, they tend to be a tawny grey.

Nocturnal, secretive, solitary creatures, cougars come together only to mate. Each cat establishes a territory of 200 to 280 sq km (125 to 175 sq mi). They favour dense forest that provides cover while hunting. They also hide among rock outcroppings and in steep canyons.

Habitat loss and aggressive predator-control programs have severely limited the range of this mysterious animal that once lived throughout North America. Still, cougars are not considered endangered or threatened. Cougars appear to be thriving in western Canada.

Cougars are carnivores. They eat everything from mice to elk but prefer deer. They occasionally stalk people but rarely

Squirrel

attack them. In folklore, cougars are called *ghost cats* or *ghost walkers*, for good reason. They're very shy and typically avoid human contact. Nevertheless, cougars have attacked solo hikers and lone cross-country skiers in the Canadian Rockies.

Cougar sightings and encounters are increasing due to a thriving cougar population, humanity's ever-expanding footprint, and the growing number of people visiting the wilderness.

If you're lucky enough to see a cougar, treasure the experience. Just remember they're unpredictable. Follow these suggestions:

• Never hike alone in areas of known cougar sightings. Keep children close to you; pick them up if you see fresh cougar scat or tracks.

• Never approach a cougar, especially a feeding one. Never flee from a cougar, or even turn your back on it. Sudden movement might trigger an instinctive attack. Avert your gaze and speak to it in a calm, soothing voice. Hold your ground or back away slowly. Always give the animal a way out.

• If a cougar approaches, spread your arms, open your jacket, do anything you can to enlarge your image. If it acts aggressively, wave your arms, shout, throw rocks or sticks. If attacked, fight back. Don't play dead.

Maps

The Gem Trek maps *Best of Jasper* and *Jasper & Maligne Lake* were our primary references while writing this book. For hiking in the Canadian Rockies, Gem Trek topographic maps (maps@gemtrek.com) are the most helpful.

The maps we created and that accompany each trip in this book are for general orientation only. Our *On Foot* directions are elaborate and precise, so referring to a topo map shouldn't be necessary. Nevertheless, you might want one.

After reaching a summit, a topo map will enable you to interpret the surrounding geography. If the terrain through which you're hiking intrigues you, a topo map can contribute to a more fulfilling experience.

The stats box for each trip indicates which Gem Trek map to bring. You can purchase them at outdoor shops and bookstores in and near the Canadian Rockies.

Carry a Compass

Left and *right* are relative. Any hiking guidebook relying solely on these inadequate and potentially misleading terms should be shredded and dropped into a recycling bin.

You'll find all the *On Foot* descriptions in this book include frequent compass directions. That's the only way to accurately, reliably guide a hiker.

What about GPS? Compared to a compass, GPS units are heavier, bulkier, more fragile, more complex, more time consuming, occasionally foiled by vegetation or topography, dependent on batteries, and way more expensive.

Keep in mind that the compass directions provided in this book are of use only if you're carrying a compass. Granted, our route descriptions are so detailed, you'll rarely have to check your compass. But bring one anyway, just in case.

A compass is required hiking equipment—anytime, anywhere, regardless of your level of experience, or your familiarity with the terrain.

Clip your compass to the shoulder strap of your pack, so you can glance at it quickly and easily. Even if you never have to rely on your compass, occasionally checking it will strengthen your sense of direction—an enjoyable, helpful, and conceivably lifesaving asset.

Keep in mind that our stated compass directions are always in reference to true north. In the Canadian Rockies, that's approximately 19° left of (counterclockwise from) magnetic north. If that puzzles, you, read your compass owner's manual.

Physical Capability

Until you gain experience judging your physical capability and that of your companions, these guidelines might be helpful. Anything longer than an 11-km (7-mi) round-trip dayhike can be very taxing for someone who doesn't hike regularly.

A 425-m (1400-ft) elevation gain in that distance is challenging but possible for anyone in average physical condition. Very fit hikers are comfortable hiking 24 km (15 mi) and ascending 1000 m (3280 ft)—or more—in a single day.

Wilderness Ethics

We hope you're already conscientious about respecting nature and other people. If not, here's how to pay off some of your karmic debt load.

Let wildflowers live. They blossom for only a few fleeting weeks. Uprooting them doesn't enhance your enjoyment, and it prevents others from seeing them at all. We once heard parents urge a string of children to pick as many different-coloured flowers as they could find. Great. Teach kids to entertain themselves by destroying nature, so the world continues marching toward environmental collapse.

Stay on the trail Shortcutting causes erosion. It doesn't save time on steep ascents, because you'll soon be slowing to catch your breath. On a steep descent, it increases the likelihood of injury. If hiking in a group across trail-less terrain, soften your impact by spreading out.

Roam meadows with your eyes, not your boots. Again, stay on the trail. If it's braided, follow the main path. When you're compelled to take a photo among wildflowers, try to walk on rocks.

Leave no trace. Be aware of your impact. Travel lightly on the land. After a rest stop, take a few minutes to look for and obscure any evidence of your stay. Restore the area to its natural state.

Wood lily

Pack out everything you bring. Never leave a scrap of trash anywhere. This includes toilet paper, nut shells, and cigarette butts. Fruit peels are also trash. They take years to decompose, and wild animals won't eat them. And don't just pack out your trash. Leave nothing behind, whether you brought it or not. Keep a small plastic bag handy, so picking up trash is easy.

Poop without impact. In the wilds, choose a site at least 60 m (66 yd) from trails and water sources. Ground that receives sunlight part of the day is best. Use a trowel to dig a small cat hole—10 to 20 cm (4 to 8 inches) deep, 10 to 15 cm (4 to 6 inches) wide—in soft, dark, biologically active soil. Afterward, throw a handful of dirt into the hole, stir with a stick to speed decomposition, replace your diggings, then camouflage the site. Pack out used toilet paper in a plastic bag. You can drop the paper (not the plastic) in the next outhouse you pass. Always clean your hands with a moisturizing hand sanitizer, like Purell. Sold in drugstores, it comes in conveniently small, lightweight, plastic bottles.

Urinate off trail, well away from water sources. The salt in urine attracts animals. They'll defoliate urine-soaked vegetation, so aim for dirt or pine needles.

Respect the reverie of other hikers. On busy trails, don't feel it's necessary to communicate with everyone you pass. Most of us are seeking solitude, not a soiree. A simple greeting is sufficient to convey good will. Obviously, only you can judge what's appropriate at the time. But it's usually presumptuous and annoying to blurt out advice without being asked. "Boy, have you got a long way to go." "The views are much better up there." "Be careful, it gets rougher." If anyone wants to know, they'll ask. Some people are sly. They start by asking where you're going, so they can tell you all about it. Offer unsolicited information only to warn other hikers about conditions ahead that could seriously affect their trip.

Hiking With Your Dog

"Can I bring Max, my Pomeranian?"

Yes. Jasper National Park allows dogs in the backcountry with the stipulation that they be leashed the entire time.

Bringing your dog hiking with you, however, isn't simply a matter of "Can I or can't I?" The larger question is "Should I or shouldn't I?"

Consider the social consequences. Most dog owners think their pets are angelic. But other hikers rarely agree.

A curious dog, even if friendly, can be a nuisance. A barking dog is annoying. A person continually yelling unheeded commands at a disobedient dog is infuriating, because it amounts to *two* annoying animals, not just one. An untrained dog, despite the owner's hearty reassurance that "he won't hurt you," can be frightening.

A well-behaved dog and his responsible owner

Consider your environmental responsibilities. Many dog owners blithely allow their pets to pollute streams and lakes. The fact that their dog is crapping in the trail doesn't occur to them, but it certainly does to the next hiker who comes along and steps in it.

Consider the safety issues. Dogs in the backcountry are a danger to themselves. For example, they could be spiked by porcupines. Even worse, they can endanger their owners and other hikers, because dogs infuriate bears. If a dog runs off, it might reel a bear back with it.

This isn't a warning not to bring your dog. We've completed lengthy trips with friends whose dogs we enjoyed immensely. This is a plea to see your dog objectively, from the perspective of your fellow hikers.

Weather

The volatile Canadian Rocky Mountain climate will have you building shrines to placate the weather gods. Conditions change quickly and dramatically. Summer is pitifully short.

Most trails aren't snow-free until mid-June. Alpine passes can be blanketed in white until mid-July. Snowfall is possible on any day, and likely at higher elevations after August. Above treeline, the annual average temperature is below freezing, and most precipitation is snow.

The Jasper Information Centre posts weather forecasts and trail-condition reports. Recorded weather forecasts are available by phone: (780) 852-6176. When the snowpack is melting in late spring and early summer, just one week of clear, sunny weather can greatly increase trail accessibility.

Regardless of the forecast, always be prepared for heavy rain, harsh winds, plummeting temperatures, sleet, hail... the whole miserable gamut. Also allow for the possibility of scorching sun and soaring temperatures. The weather can change drasti-cally, with alarming speed. Though the sky is clear at dawn,

Summer storm

it might be boiling with ominous black clouds by afternoon. Storms can dissipate equally fast.

Statistics indicate that, throughout the Canadian Rockies, you can expect rainfall one of every three days in summer. Even many rain-free days are cloudy. So don't squander a blue sky. Celebrate it: hike fast and far.

Charts showing Jasper Park's average monthly precipitation during hiking season are of little help. June is likely to be wettest, October driest. The figures for July, August and September are too close for anyone to reliably recommend when your hiking trip is least likely to be rained out. Locals, however, will tell you that we usually get a snowstorm in early September, followed by a couple weeks of clear skies, pleasantly cool daytime temperatures, and nighttime lows around freezing.

Charts showing the average monthly maximum and minimum temperatures in the mountain parks reveal the following.

By May the highs reach about 16°C (61°F), the lows stay just above freezing. In June, the highs and lows are roughly 4°C (7°F) warmer than in May. July is usually the hottest month, with highs around 24°C (75°F), lows averaging 7°C (45°F). August can be almost as hot as July, but generally isn't. September tends to be slightly warmer than May. In October, the highs top out near 12°C (54°F), the lows drop just below freezing.

Fall is touted by many as the ideal time to hike in the Canadian Rockies. Bugs are absent, crowds diminish, the larch trees are golden. But by then the sun is rising later and setting earlier, which restricts dayhiking. We prefer the long days of mid-summer.

Typically, the Canadian Rocky Mountain climate will grant you about two-and-a-half months of optimal high-country hiking. That's only 20% of the year. At the end of June, however, you'll have 16½ hours between sunrise (5:30 a.m.) and sunset (10 p.m.).

Carpe diem.

Lightning

Many of the trails in this book lead to meadows and ridges where, during a storm, you could be exposed to lightning.

Storms tend to develop in the afternoon, so you can try to reach alpine destinations early in the day. But it's impossible to always evade violent weather. You hike to commune with nature, the power of which can threaten your safety.

Even if you start under a cloudless, blue sky, you might see ominous, black thunderheads marching toward you a few hours later. Upon reaching a high, airy vantage, you could be forced by an approaching storm to decide if and when you should retreat to safer ground.

The following is a summary of lightning precautions recommended by experts. These are not guaranteed solutions. We offer them merely as suggestions to help you make wise choices and reduce your chance of injury.

If your hair is standing on end, there's electricity in the air around you. A lightning strike could be imminent. Get outa there! That's usually down the mountain, but if there's too much open expanse to traverse, look for closer protection.

A direct lightning strike can kill you. It can cause brain damage, heart failure or third-degree burns. Ground current, from a nearby strike, can severely injure you, causing deep burns and tissue damage. Direct strikes are worse, but ground-current contact is far more common.

Avoid a direct strike by getting off exposed ridges and peaks. Even a few meters (yards) off a ridge is better than on top. Avoid isolated, tall trees. A clump of small trees or an opening in the trees is safer.

Avoid ground current by getting out of stream gullies and away from crevices, lichen patches, or wet, solid-rock surfaces. Loose rock, like talus, is safer.

Look for a low-risk area, near a highpoint at least 10 m/yd higher than you. Crouch near its base, at least 1.5 m/yd from cliffs or walls.

Once you choose a place to wait it out, your goal is to prevent brain or heart damage by stopping an electrical charge from flowing through your whole body. Squat with your boots touching one another. If you have a sleeping pad, put it beneath your boots for insulation. Keep your hands away from rocks. Fold your arms across your chest. Stay at least 10 m/yd from your companions, so if one is hit, another can give cardiopulmonary resuscitation.

Deep caves offer protection. Crouch away from the mouth, at least 1.5 m/yd from the walls. But avoid rock overhangs and shallow depressions, because ground current can jump across them. Lacking a deep cave, you're safer in the low-risk area below a highpoint.

Hypothermia

Many deaths outdoors involve no obvious injury. "Exposure" is usually cited as the killer, but that's a misleading term. It vaguely refers to conditions related to the hikers' demise.

The actual cause is hypothermia: excessive loss of body heat. It can happen with startling speed, in surprisingly mild weather—often between 0 and 10°C (30 and 50°F). Guard against it vigilantly.

Cool temperatures, moisture (perspiration or rain), wind, or fatigue, usually a combination, sap the body of vital warmth. Hypothermia results when heat loss continues to exceed heat gain.

Initial symptoms include chills and shivering. Poor coordination, slurred speech, sluggish thinking, and memory loss are next.

Intense shivering then decreases while muscular rigidity increases, accompanied by irrationality, incoherence, even hallucinations. Stupor, blue skin, slowed pulse and respiration, and unconsciousness follow. The heartbeat finally becomes erratic until the victim dies.

Avoid becoming hypothermic by wearing synthetic clothing that wicks moisture away from your skin and insulates when wet. Read *Prepare For Your Hike*, in the back of this book, for a description of clothing and equipment that will help you stay warm and dry.

Food fuels your internal fire, so bring more than you think you'll need, including several energy bars for emergencies only.

If you can't stay warm and dry, you must escape the wind and rain. Turn back. Keep moving. Eat snacks. Seek shelter. Do it while you're still mentally and physically capable.

Snow is possible even in summer.

Watch others in your party for signs of hypothermia. Victims might resist help at first. Trust the symptoms, not the person. Be insistent. Act immediately.

Create the best possible shelter for the victim. Take off his wet clothes and replace them with dry ones. Insulate him from the ground. Provide warmth. Build a fire. Keep the victim conscious. Feed him sweets. Carbohydrates quickly convert to heat and energy. In advanced cases, victims should not drink hot liquids.

Mt. Edith Cavell and Cavell Lake

done in a day

the hikes

trip 1
beaver, summit and jacques lakes

location	off Maligne Lake Road, north of Medicine Lake
round trip	9.6 km (6 mi) to first Summit Lake 22.4 km (13.9 mi) to Jacques Lake
elevation gain	77 m (253 ft) to first Summit Lake 109 m (358 ft) round trip to Jacques
key elevations	trailhead 1450 m (4756 ft) first Summit Lake 1527 m (5010 ft) Jacques Lake 1495 m (4904 ft)
hiking time	2½ to 3½ hours for first Summit Lake 5 to 7 hours for Jacques Lake
difficulty	easy
available	early May through October
map	Gem Trek *Jasper and Maligne Lake*

opinion

The trail to Jacques Lake is about as level as this sentence. It travels a long, narrow valley, deep in forest. En route you'll follow a creek and visit several lesser lakes: Beaver, the two Summit Lakes, and an unnamed fourth.

Though much of the way is treed, you'll occasionally lift your eyes to the soaring sawtooth ridges of the Queen Elizabeth Ranges. What you're unlikely to see here is a crowd, making this trail a fine choice for a quiet walk in the woods.

When the alplands are snow splattered in late fall, and you're wondering "what now?" Jacques could be the answer. The creek crossings beyond the second Summit Lake are insignificant then, and the entire valley is less muddy.

Beaver Lake and the Queen Elizabeth Ranges

Also keep this hike in mind for a rainy day. Even if clouds are banging into the peaks, you'll glimpse mountain walls. And the threat of a lightning strike in such a sheltered valley is minimal.

Admittedly, the trail to Jacques is most enjoyable in summer, when the valley is idyllically green and warm breezes invite languorous lakeside lounging. But strong, adventurous hikers should be rocketing into the alpine zone then, fully relishing the Canadian Rockies' unique grandeur.

Though smaller, the Summit Lakes are as enjoyable as Jacques. Their pebble beaches are spacious. And the airy, cottonwood poplars ringing their shores are a welcome change from pines, especially in fall when the leaves are golden.

On a sunny October afternoon, this is a good place to conceive the book you want to write, ponder names for your baby-to-be, list the qualities you want in a mate, or, if you're tired of thinking, watch the loons or Harlequin ducks play.

The shallow Summit Lakes recede substantially by late summer. Curiously, no creek appears to connect them. An underground stream is the umbilical cord.

Beaver Lake is an ideal destination for parents eager to introduce toddlers to hiking. Adults can reach this first lake in 20 minutes. With an inquisitive little one meandering to examine leaves and rocks, it might take an hour or more.

Ideally, hike at least to the first Summit Lake—about a three-hour round trip. The forest opens here. The meadow at the south shore affords views of the surrounding high country. In spring, you can expect a colourful wildflower display comprising yellow avens, lavender bluebells, and pink wild roses.

The attraction of Jacques Lake is its wilderness atmosphere, not dramatic scenery. So if you feel like turning around at the first Summit Lake, do so without concern of missing a climactic destination. The view is more expansive at the first Summit Lake than it is at the second. It's still another hour through forest to Jacques.

fact

before your trip

Want to captain a rowboat on Beaver Lake? Call Curries Guided Fishing: (780-852-5650). Visit them at Source for Sports, 416 Patricia Street, Jasper. The boats are locked on the lakeshore, so you'll have to get a key.

by vehicle

From the junction with Connaught Drive at the north end of Jasper townsite, drive Hwy 16 north 1.8 km (1.1 mi). Turn right (east) onto Maligne Lake Road (signed for Jasper Park Lodge), cross the Athabasca River bridge, then go left (north-northeast). Proceed 27.5 km (17.1 mi) and turn left (north) into the Beaver Creek picnic area. It's across from the south end of Medicine Lake. Elevation: 1450 m (4756 ft).

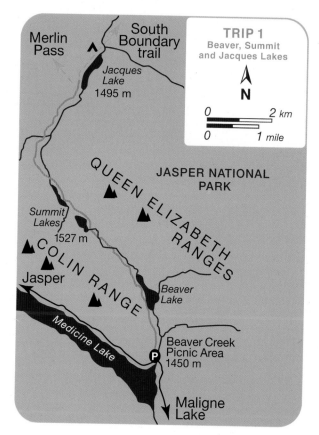

on foot

A gated fire road departs the northeast corner of the parking area. Follow it north. Cross the bridged creek. Soon pass a ranger cabin on the right. A few minutes farther, the road parallels the creek. It then ascends gently.

About seven minutes from the trailhead, the road levels, still heading generally north. The creek (about 21 m / 70 ft below the road) is audible.

Summit Lake and the southeast end of the Colin Range

Within 20 minutes, having gained just 32 m (105 ft), reach the south end of **Beaver Lake** at 1.6 km (1 mi). There's a picnic table, firepit and outhouse here, as well as the aforementioned rowboats.

The road continues north-northwest along the west shore for five minutes. It then pulls away from the water briefly before passing the lake's north end and heading northwest. An open willow patch unveils an impressive peak to the right (west).

Attain open views about an hour from the trailhead. The mountains behind you (southeast) are now visible, in addition to the sheer, gray, Queen Elizabeth Ranges nearby right (west) where a cascade cleaves a high gully. From here on, the road is narrower, more overgrown.

Reach a junction at 4.8 km (3 mi), 1527 m (5010 ft). The right fork, signed for the South Boundary Trail, continues past the Summit Lakes to Jacques Lake, but there's a quicker, more scenic option: proceed straight (slightly left) and soon arrive at the meadowy south end of the **first Summit Lake.** Visible up-valley (northwest) is 2820-m (9250-ft) Sirdar Mtn.

A faint path rounds the right (northeast) shore. This is the shortcut. When it fades at the north end of the first Summit Lake, simply continue northwest five minutes through forest to the smaller, narrower, second Summit Lake.

Prefer the official trail? From the meadowy south end of the first Summit Lake, retrace your steps to the junction. Follow the signed South Boundary Trail, which skirts the northeast side of the first Summit Lake, well back from the shore.

Rough and narrow, the trail undulates through tight forest, crossing several streamlets (possibly dry in fall). After descending from a small rise, reach the **second Summit Lake** at 6 km (3.7 mi). Fast hikers will arrive here about 20 minutes after leaving the junction.

Regardless which way you arrived at the second Summit Lake, if continuing to Jacques Lake, follow the South Boundary Trail northwest around the right (northeast) shore of the second Summit Lake.

At 7.4 km (4.6 mi) skirt left of yet another tiny lake, then face several minor stream crossings. The trail gradually bends northeast.

Returning from Summit Lakes

Reach a junction at 11 km (6.8 mi). Left (northwest) leads to Merlin Pass. Proceed straight to reach the south end of **Jacques Lake** at 11.2 km (7 mi), 1495 m (4904 ft).

trip 2

angel glacier / cavell meadows

location	south of Jasper townsite
	end of Mt. Edith Cavell Road
circuit	6.1 km (3.8 mi) to 7.9 km (4.9 mi)
elevation gain	385 m (1263 ft) to 523 m (1716 ft)
key elevations	trailhead 1765 m (5790 ft)
	highpoint 2288 m (7507 ft)
hiking time	2 to 3 hours
difficulty	easy
available	mid-July through September
map	Gem Trek *Jasper National Park*

opinion

Wildflower meadows are like coral reefs. Both are so visually arresting, they can rivet our attention to the present moment.

That's why hiking or snorkeling feel cathartic. They sever our debilitating preoccupation with the past and future. Suddenly we're fully awake—fascinated, enchanted—actually living instead of merely remembering or imagining.

Ready for some here-and-now therapy? Hike to Cavell Meadows. During full bloom (late July through August) they're a riot of colour, as brilliantly and variously hued as a reef teeming with tropical fish.

If your timing is fortunate, your eyes will swim through bold splashes of red, pink, yellow, purple and white. If not, you'll still see Angel Glacier clinging to the north face of Mt. Edith Cavell. It's one of many compelling spectacles that earned Jasper National Park recognition as a UNESCO World

Angel Glacier

Heritage Site. You'll see it constantly en route to the natural grandstand of Cavell Meadows.

The famous winged glacier is, of course, high on the must-see list of most Jasper visitors. To witness it in solitude, come very early or late in the day. Otherwise leather-sheathed bikers, motorhome muffins, and eager kids towing parents will likely join you on this easy excursion. So wear a smile, and post a sentry before stopping to pee.

Snarly weather discourages most people yet often enhances close-range scenery by creating atmosphere. The crowd won't be here then; maybe you should be. The flower-rich, heather meadows are impressive rain or shine. Angel Glacier, draped over a 300-m (984-ft) cliff, can be more alluring wreathed in clouds.

Serious hikers seeking a wilderness experience should invest the couple hours they'd spend here on a more adventurous trip, like Geraldine Lakes (Trip 8), Verdant Pass (Trip 9), or Campus Pass (Trip 10).

Angel Glacier, Cavell Meadows, and 3363-m (11,033-ft) Mt. Edith Cavell were named in honour of a British nurse who helped hundreds of allied soldiers escape German-occupied Belgium during WWI. Her subsequent execution garnered sympathetic media coverage worldwide. So Angel Glacier is a reminder: angels are real, and the world needs more of them.

fact

before your trip

Ask the Jasper Info Centre about current conditions at Cavell Meadows. To safeguard sensitive subalpine and alpine vegetation, hiking might be restricted here until mid-July, when the meadows are snowfree.

But even if the extended trail is closed, a 1.8-km (1.1-mi) loop—partly paved, known as the *Path of the Glacier trail*—remains open and affords views of Angel Glacier.

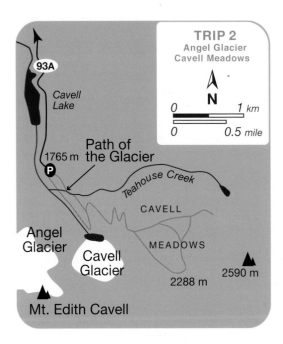

Remind everyone in your group to stay on the trail. Be especially vigilant about this with children. Explain why, so they understand: meadows are quickly, easily trampled, and the short growing season near and above treeline prevents recovery, thus the damage is permanent.

More than 45,000 people visit Cavell Meadows each summer. Many wander off trail, either thoughtlessly shortcutting or inanely attempting to keep their footwear out of the mud.

The Friends of Jasper, Parks Canada, and local residents have worked to restore and protect the meadows. They've rerouted sections of trail, improved drainage, erected signs displaying maps, and blocked or rehabilitated 50 ad hoc paths.

With the official trail now obvious, and the temptation to hike off-trail reduced, the meadows are slowly recovering.

Visit www.friendsofjasper.com/projects/cavell.htm to see before-and-after photos of Cavell Meadows and read trail updates.

by vehicle

From the junction of Hwy 16 and the Icefields Parkway (Hwy 93), at the southwest edge of Jasper townsite, drive the Parkway south 7.2 km (4.5 mi). Turn right (west) onto Hwy 93A. At 9.7 km (6 mi), stay left on Hwy 93A where Marmot Basin Road forks right. At 12.5 km (7.8 mi) turn right onto Mt. Edith Cavell Road. (The parking lot here is for trailers and large RVs, which the narrow, winding road ahead does not accommodate.) Pass the youth hostel (left) at 17.4 km (10.8 mi). Just beyond, pass the Astoria River / Tonquin Valley trailhead parking lot (right). At 27 km (16.7 mi) enter the Angel Glacier / Cavell Meadows trailhead parking lot at road's end. Elevation: 1765 m (5790 ft).

on foot

Start on the left (east) arm of the paved **Path of the Glacier trail.** It departs the southwest corner of the parking lot. Initially follow either the steps or the gently ascending path. They rejoin just uphill.

Pavement ends within ten minutes. Proceed on the dirt-and-gravel trail. Reach a **junction** at 0.5 km (0.3 mi). The Path of the Glacier trail goes right (southeast), returning to the parking lot to complete a 1.8-km (1.1-mi) loop. Turn left (north-northeast) onto the Cavell Meadows trail.

Switchback up over a lateral moraine. At 1.4 km (0.9 mi), about 20 minutes above the junction, attain the first full view of **Angel Glacier**. The pond below the glacier's toe is also visible. The trail then climbs steeply through subalpine forest, granting occasional glimpses of the glacier.

Reach the next **junction** at 2 km (1.2 mi). You'll return here on the Cavell Meadows circuit. Go right (southeast) for the easiest

Cavell Meadows are profuse with wildflowers

ascent. Soon enter the **meadows.** In July you'll likely see yellow glacier-lilies, golden marsh marigolds, and white globeflowers.

The ascent continues. Mt. Edith Cavell and Angel Glacier are prominently visible. From this higher vantage, the wings look less angelic because it's now apparent the right one is shorter and bulkier.

At 2.8 km (1.7 mi), 2065 m (6775 ft), reach a **fork** at the south end of the meadow circuit. Right (east-southeast), a cairned spur leads one minute to a viewpoint. Turn left to ascend north and continue the circuit.

Reach a **junction** at 3 km (1.9 mi), 2150 m (7054 ft). Left descends north, offering the shortest possible meadow circuit. To continue the full circuit, ascend right.

At 3.4 km (2.1 mi), 2200 m (7218 ft), reach another junction. Left (west) is the return leg of the circuit. Right (northeast) is

Globeflower

a spur leading to the east end of the circuit: a **climactic viewpoint** at 3.9 km (2.4 mi), 2288 m (7507 ft).

After admiring the vista, descend to the previous junction. Bear right (west) and begin the return leg of the circuit. Soon bear right again at the next junction.

At 5.1 km (3.2 mi) reach the junction where you began the circuit. You're now on familiar ground. Bear right and descend back to the moraine.

Rejoin the **Path of the Glacier trail** at 6.6 km (4.1 mi). Go right (northwest) to arrive at the trailhead in ten minutes. Or, lengthen your hike (reaching the trailhead in 25 minutes) by going left (southeast).

Taking the longer option, you'll skirt the **pond** below the glacier's toe in 0.5 km (0.3 mi) then descend northwest to arrive at the parking lot, where your total distance will be 7.9 km (4.9 mi).

trip 3
celestine lake / devona lookout

location	north of Jasper Lake, at the end of Celestine Lake Road
round trip	14 km (8.7 mi) to Celestine Lake
	19.2 km (11.9 mi) to Devona Lookout
elevation gain	161 m (528 ft) to Celestine Lake
	330 m (1082 ft) to Devona Lookout
key elevations	trailhead 1080 m (3542 ft)
	lake 1241 m (4072 ft)
	lookout 1410 m (4625 ft)
hiking time	4½ to 6 hours
difficulty	easy
available	May through October
map	Gem Trek *Jasper and Maligne Lake*

opinion

By mid-summer, most hikers would scoff at the suggestion of walking an old road, mostly through forest, to attain a view of a valley pierced by a major highway.

But in early spring, striding beyond pavement in the Canadian Rockies without post-holing through ice-crusted snow can be a jubilant experience. That's when Celestine Lake and Devona Lookout beckon.

Their invitation is also appealing in late autumn, when a sudden blizzard can turn an alpine hike into an ordeal ranging anywhere from shiver-fest to blind man's bluff.

Princess and Celestine lakes are shrouded in forest, unadorned by cliffy backdrops. Devona Lookout grants a panoramic view of the Athabasca River Valley, including Roche Miette, but it's only a marginal improvement on what you'll see en route to the trailhead.

So don't come here outside shoulder season, when more rewarding, higher-elevation trails like Bald Hills (Trip 6) or Verdant Pass (Trip 9) are available. Violate that edict only to herd children on an easy, summer backpack trip to Celestine Lake's pleasant campground.

Cycling here is an option. But on a fat-tire bike, you'll quickly dispatch the short distance, thus defeating the purpose of spending time outdoors in shoulder season.

This trip is better indulged on foot, either in May, June, or October. Though you'll be walking a road, you'll appreciate that it grants a broad, scenic passage through this exceptionally pretty forest of primarily aspen and Douglas fir.

The sun liberally penetrates the open canopy to nourish tall, emerald grass and a plethora of wildflowers: lavender camas lily, yellow shrubby cinquefoil, white daisies, Indian paintbrush, lavender harebells, pink clover. The large bunches of complex, red-orange wood lilies that flourish here are a rare treat in the Canadian Rockies.

Another attraction of this hike is the drive to the trailhead. The 28-km (17.5-mi) Celestine Lake Road plies the west side of the broad Athabasca River Valley, climbing high enough to afford grand views of open, tranquil, montane country.

The road feels remote because it's single lane and mostly unpaved, but Jasper Lake—slender, shallow, placid—is all that separates it from the whoosh and whine of RVs and transport trucks on the Yellowhead Hwy.

Because the Celestine Lake Road is narrow, one-way travel is necessary to prevent collisions. The direction of travel alternates for one-hour periods throughout the day. You'll find the schedule posted on the road and listed below.

Returning from Celestine Lake

Snaring River campground is an inviting place to spend the night before or after your Devona Lookout hike. You'll also pass a couple small tentsites on the Celestine Lake Road. Their location is indicated in the by vehicle directions below.

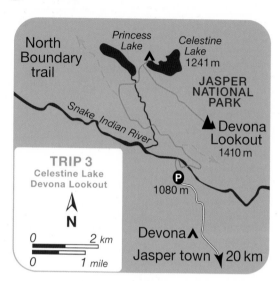

fact

before your trip

From downtown Jasper, allow at least 45 minutes to reach the traffic-regulated section of the Celestine Lake Road. Below are the hours designated for one-way travel. Confirm with the Jasper Info Centre, or simply wait to read the sign on the road.

Inbound (north) one-way travel

8 to 9 am, 11 to 12 noon, 2 to 3 pm, 5 to 6 pm, 8 to 9 pm

Outbound (south) one-way travel

9:30 to 10:30 am, 12:30 to 1:30 pm, 3:30 to 4:30 pm, 6:30 to 7:30 pm

Though narrow and winding, the Celestine Lake Road is passable in a 2WD car. But don't try it in an RV or with a trailer. Slow down on blind curves. Use your horn for safety.

Celestine Lake road

by vehicle

From Jasper townsite, drive north on Hwy 16. Pass the turnoff for Jasper Park Lodge (at the large, metal bridge) and continue 7.6 km (4.7 mi). Turn left (west) onto the road signed for Snaring River campground. Set your trip odometer to 0.

100 m (110 yd)
Drive beneath the railroad trestle. Bear right.

5.1 km (3.2 mi)
Pass Snaring River campground (left), then cross a bridge.

5.5 km (3.4 mi)
Pass the overflow camping area (right).

6.3 km (3.9 mi)
The road curves left and is unpaved beyond. A sign here states the one-way schedule. (The road does not end at 19 km as indicated.)

11.5 km (7.1 mi)
Pass the Moberly homestead (right).

12.6 km (7.8 mi)
Pass the warden's residence (left). Proceed generally northeast.

14 km (8.7 mi)
One-way travel begins here. Obey the posted times. Cross the Corral Creek bridge. The road beyond has tighter curves, but remains well graded.

14.5 km (9 mi)
Pass Pretty Creek campground (right). No fee is required to stay here. There's room for a couple vehicles and tents.

15.5 km (9.6 mi)
Cross a narrow, rough bridge.

15.7 km (9.7 mi)
Cross Vine Creek bridge.

17.5 km (10.9 mi)
The road curves around a point, high on a slope.

26 km (16.1 mi)
Pass Devona campground (left). No fee is required to stay here. There's room for one vehicle and a tent.

28 km (17.4 mi)
Reach the trailhead parking lot, at 1080 m (3542 ft). The road is gated beyond.

on foot

The North Boundary Trail begins here. Past the 5.2-km (3.2-mi) junction, it's almost entirely in forest. Cycling is permitted only as far as Snake Indian Falls, at 26.5 km (16.4 mi).

From the gate, the road descends to an iron bridge spanning **Snake Indian River** at 0.5 km (0.3 mi).

On the far bank, a sweeping curve ascends a steep slope. Atop the bench, abundant sunshine enables huge Douglas firs to attain impressive height and girth.

Celestine Lake

Your general direction of travel is now northwest and will remain so to Celestine junction. The ascent is gradual the entire way.

For about 15 minutes, enjoy open views left (west) across the Snake Indian River valley to the De Smet Range, and ahead (northwest) into the heavily forested North Boundary country.

At 5.2 km (3.2 mi), 1245 m (4084 ft), reach a signed **junction** in a clearing. The North Boundary Trail proceeds straight (northwest), reaching Mt. Robson in 180 km (112 mi). Go right (north, then northeast) for Celestine Lake.

The ascent is minimal. From a small rise, descend a bit. At 6.7 km (4.2 mi) a short spur forks left to the southeast shore of 1.5-km (0.9-mi) long, forest-enclosed **Princess Lake.** There's no place to sit on the shore. The Beaver Bluffs rise behind it (north).

Back on the main road/trail, continue 100 m (110 yd) to a fork. Left descends north, quickly ending on the west shore of **Celestine Lake** at 7 km (4.2 mi), 1241 m (4072 ft). Straight ascends southeast to Devona Lookout.

Lacking large boulders to sit on, the water's edge at Celestine Lake is unaccommodating. But among the spruce trees, just above the shore, is a small **campground** with five tentsites. The tables provide a comfortable vantage. There's also an out-house, fire pit, and bear-proof food storage.

From where the road/trail forks at Celestine Lake, straight leads southeast to Devona Lookout. It's narrow, overgrown, ascending moderately along a gentle, forested ridge.

In about 2 km (1.2 mi), at 1363 m (4472 ft), attain views on the right (southwest). Reach the **Devona Lookout,** or rather its former site, at 9.6 km (6 mi), 1410 m (4625 ft). Proceed straight ahead, downhill slightly, for better views.

Jasper Lake is south. East, across the Athabasca River Valley and Hwy 16, is 2315-m (7593-ft) Roche Miette. The Miette Range builds southeast beyond it.

The Rocky River Valley, paralleling the south slope of the Miette Range, burned in the summer of 2003. The fire was intentionally started by the Park service as a "controlled burn." It consumed much of the valley, well up the South Boundary Trail.

Wild Chives

trip 4
opal hills

location	end of Maligne Lake Road immediately north of Maligne Lake
circuit	8.2 km (5.1 mi)
elevation gain	460 m (1500 ft)
key elevations	trailhead 1700 m (5576 ft) highpoint 2160 m (7085 ft)
hiking time	3 to 4 hours
difficulty	moderate
available	mid-July through late September
map	Gem Trek *Jasper & Maligne Lake*

opinion

If these hills are alive with music, you'll hear it all, from the swooning melodrama of an orchestral movie score, to the intimate honesty of a solo aboriginal shaman playing an eagle-bone whistle. Because hiking up the Opal Hills, you'll see it all, from vast, turquoise, mountain-squeezed Maligne Lake, to diminutive wildflowers clinging to life in the rock and tundra.

King gentian

Come on up. Nestle in the lee of a slope. Luxuriate in the greenery and tranquility. Gaze at the distant Rocky Mountain horizon. Maybe soak up some sun. Or go hunting; in the dales between the hills lurk rare, indigo-coloured, waxy king gentian.

Intrepid wallflower

Maligne Lake and Mounts Unwin and Charlton, from Opal Hills

To get there, however, you must lay siege to these steep hills. The ascent lacks switchbacks, so it's slippery when wet. But it's short enough that most hikers won't complain. Just don't go on a rainy day, when the trail is laundry-chute slick, and you'll be deprive d of the rapturous view over Maligne Lake.

fact

by vehicle

From the junction with Connaught Drive at the north end of Jasper townsite, drive Hwy 16 north 1.8 km (1.1 mi). Turn right (east) onto Maligne Lake Road (signed for Jasper Park Lodge), cross the Athabasca River bridge, then go left (north-north-east). Proceed 45 km (28 mi) to Maligne Lake. Turn left into the main parking area, just before the lodge. Stay left to reach the third and highest lot, at 1700 m (5576 ft).

on foot

In 200 m (220 yd) stay left where the Maligne Lakeshore trail forks right. Begin a steep ascent northeast through lodgepole pine forest.

Jasper

Maligne Lake Road

OPAL HILLS

2160 m

1700 m P

lodge ↑

Mary
Schaffer
Loop

Maligne
Lake

P

Bald
Hills

*Tall white
bog orchid*

TRIP 4
Opal Hills

N

0   1 km
0   0.5 mile

At the 1.6-km (1-mi) **junction**, where the Opal Hills loop begins, bear right and continue northeast. Ascending moderately, the trail gradually curves northwest.

At 2.6 km (1.6 mi) reach alpine meadows. At 3.2 km (2 mi), attain the loop **highpoint**: 2160 m (7085 ft).

Ascend one of the grassy hills for a view southeast over Maligne Lake and to glacier-laden Mts. Charlton and Unwin. The Bald Hills (Trip 6) are visible southwest across the valley.

From the highpoint, proceed through gentle meadowland between low hills. The trail gradually curves southeast. At 4.7 km (2.9 mi) the trail leaves the meadows and hills and descends into forest.

At 6.6 km (4.1 mi) arrive back at the loop junction. Go right (southwest) to return to the trailhead and complete the 8.2-km (5.1-mi) circuit.

trip 5

⊗ sulphur skyline

location	south of Jasper Park's East Gate end of Miette Hot Springs Road
round trip	8 km (5 mi)
elevation gain	636 m (2086 ft)
key elevations	trailhead 1380 m (4524 ft) summit 2016 m (6612 ft)
hiking time	3 hours
difficulty	moderate due only to steepness
available	April through mid-October
map	Gem Trek *Jasper & Maligne Lake*

opinion

You are a sensual creature. Your nose can catch the scent of berries in a forest, so you won't starve. Your ears can detect the distant snap of a twig, granting you a head start on a predator. Your eyes can leap far ahead of your feet, helping you bound across boulders without falling.

But modern life—motionless work, cubicles, recycled air, artificial light—deprives your senses.

What we all need, every summer, is a retreat. A celebration of our sensuality and a reminder to cultivate it. In Jasper National Park, an ideal destination for a quick retreat is Sulphur Skyline.

Steep but not far, the Sulphur Skyline trail leads to a gratifying summit panorama. You can peer deep into remote valleys and appreciate nearby sharp-edged peaks. You can survey a vast expanse devoid of human contrivances. The scenery is so wild it might rekindle cellular memories of prehistoric ancestors who sought vantage points like this to ensure their survival.

Fiddle River valley, from Sulphur Skyline summit

Your own survival, however, is assured. The trail is nearly road-width the entire way. It's tennis-shoe smooth, too, until near the rocky summit. Numerous benches en route invite you to stop, relax, and realize you really should go hiking more often.

The trip begins at the popular Miette Hot Springs. A steady stream of people waddle up here before or after their soak, though many turn back—bested by the unrelenting steep grade—well below the summit.

To attain serenity, try the usual tactics. An early start might grant you a peaceful ascent. Set out in the afternoon, and others will have departed the summit by the time you arrive. Weekdays are always less busy than weekends.

The mountain's easterly location and the trail's exposure to the sun make this one of Jasper Park's earliest snow-free hiking options. For those same reasons, it can also be mercilessly hot on a sunny, summer day. Start hydrated and pack a couple liters of water per person. Sulphur Skyline is an appealing destination in fall, too, but remember: the approach road usually closes in mid-October.

fact

by vehicle

From the junction of Hwy 16 and the Icefields Parkway, at the southwest edge of Jasper townsite, drive Hwy 16 northeast 44.3 km (27.5 mi). Or, from Jasper Park's East Gate, drive Hwy 16 southwest 7 km (4.3 mi).

From either approach, turn southeast onto Miette Hot Springs Road. Continue 17 km (10.5 mi) to the road's end parking lot, at 1370 m (4490 ft).

on foot

From the parking lot, walk up to the hot springs pool building. The entrance and passenger-dropoff loop are on the building's south side. The trail—initially a paved path—departs the east side of this loop, between the trailhead sign (left) and an info kiosk (right).

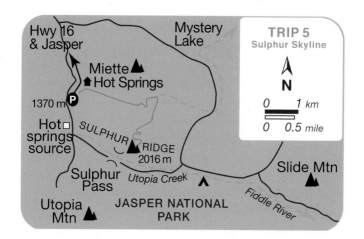

The elevation here is 1380 m (4524 ft). The sign states: Sulphur Ridge 5 km, Mystery Lake 12 km. Follow the path east and begin a gradual ascent.

Within five minutes, a paved path forks left (north-northeast) to a water tank. Proceed straight (east) on the main trail. It's unpaved from here on, but remains broad and smooth. A minute farther, ignore the horse trail branching left to a bridged stream crossing. Proceed straight (east), uphill.

The trail soon steepens, curving southeast. Cross a stream in a culvert and pass a bench blocking a defunct path. This is the first of more than a dozen benches en route to the summit. The eastward ascent steepens.

Soon, Sulphur Skyline ridge is visible right (southeast). About 30 minutes from the trailhead, pass the third bench. It affords an unobstructed view south, across a forested basin, to the Skyline.

Within 40 minutes reach a junction in **Shuey Pass** at 2.2 km (1.4 m), 1638 m (5374 ft). Left (northeast) descends to Fiddle River then continues to Mystery Lake. Go right (east) to resume the Skyline ascent. Soon attain views northeast, beyond the Yellowhead Hwy.

On Sulphur Skyline

Stay on the main trail, ignoring occasional spurs. These narrow, bootbeaten shortcuts deface the mountain and are way too steep to be helpful.

After hiking about an hour and gaining 440 m (1443 ft), get a glimpse into the valley southeast. Just ten minutes farther, the trail levels at 1896 m (6220 ft) on a **broad shoulder** beneath the summit. There's a big, prominent, white boulder here. Numerous benches invite you to appreciate the grand panorama (southeast, north, and west).

Beyond the shoulder, the trail steepens dramatically. Expect insecure footing on loose rock. Swift hikers will stride onto the flat, spacious, 2016-m (6612-ft) **summit** within 1½ hours of leaving the trailhead. Total distance: 4 km (2.5 mi).

The 360° view is captivating. Utopia Mtn is close-by southwest. The Miette Range runs northwest. Across from it is sawtoothed Ashlar Ridge. You can also see a long way up the Fiddle River valley (southeast).

It's possible to continue hiking west, out Skyline Ridge. Lower than the summit, with a diminished view, it compensates by attracting virtually no one and therefore offering tranquility.

A speedy, nonstop descent to the parking lot takes about 40 minutes.

trip 6
⊕ bald hills

location	end of Maligne Lake Road immediately west of Maligne Lake
round trip	10.2 km (6.3 mi) for lookout site and second summit via cutoff trail
elevation gain	630 m (2067 ft) to second summit
key elevations	trailhead 1690 m (5543 ft) Bald Hills lookout site 2170 m (7117 ft) second summit 2320 m (7610 ft)
hiking time	3½ hours for lookout site and second summit via cutoff trail 5 hours or more for ridgecrest beyond second summit
difficulty	easy to second summit moderate for ridgecrest
available	late June through early October
map	Gem Trek *Jasper & Maligne Lake*

opinion

Baldness is greatly admired among certain factions. Neo-Nazis. Parents of newborns. Fans of Shrek. And hikers—because a bald summit makes an excellent grandstand.

The Bald Hills in particular offer a panoramic reward way out of proportion to the trifling effort required to ascend them. You'll see razorback ridges, silver and grey, above the immense turquoise majesty of Maligne Lake (see photo on page 4). Many of the peaks look like cresting tsunami waves in a petrified sea. One monster mountain is swirled, forming a pipeline. Come see for yourself.

Cairn on the second bald hill

This destination, more than any other, screams "Jasper!" It's even better than Opal Hills (Trip 4), because here your eyes can gobble all of Maligne Lake and the Queen Elizabeth Ranges.

Gleaming white glaciers southeast are a foil for the desolate rock faces and deep green forests that complete the scene. Northwest are the expansive alpine meadowlands sliced by the Skyline trail. You can also peer southwest into Evelyn Creek valley and wonder how many bears are roaming that lonely refuge.

The name *Bald Hills* refers only to the absence of trees. The hills aren't totally bald, just buzzcut. They're adorned with heather and, in July and August, dappled with wildflowers. Look for dark-purple gentian, yellow stonecrop, lavender bellflowers, and fuchsia moss-campion.

A dusty, tiresome road leads you up the hills. On a clear summer day, it's hot as a tin roof. You can abandon the road, however, about 45 minutes up, where a cutoff trail branches left. The trail is steeper, but more pleasant and less busy. It ascends open forest and heathery slopes. Definitely take the trail down, departing near the hitching posts.

It's a short hike to the top of the first baldy. From there you can wander all day. The Bald Hills are actually a ridge, 7 km (4.3 mi) long, hikeable as far south as the the main Maligne Range. For a full day up here, be a camel: carry at least 2 liters (quarts) of water per person. You'll find none en route.

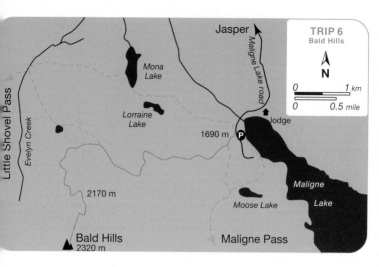

fact

by vehicle

From the junction with Connaught Drive at the north end of Jasper townsite, drive Hwy 16 north 1.8 km (1.1 mi). Turn right (east) onto Maligne Lake Road (signed for Jasper Park Lodge), cross the Athabasca River bridge, then go left (north-northeast). Proceed 45 km (28 mi) to Maligne Lake. Continue past the lodge to the parking lot at road's end. Elevation: 1690 m (5543 ft). The trailhead is at the signed, gated, dirt road across from the lot.

on foot

Set out on the broad fire road, heading generally west. Within ten minutes, proceed straight on the road, passing a signed trail left (south) to Moose Lake and Maligne Pass.

At 2.5 km (1.6 mi), 1918 m (6290 ft), the **cutoff trail** forks left. You'll surmount the first Bald Hill in 35 to 50 minutes via the short, steep trail. Figure 45 to 60 minutes via the road, because it's longer and ascends more gradually.

*Alpine
forget-me-not*

If you opt for the trail, you'll intersect the road at 4 km (2.6 mi).
Turn right. In 70 m (77 yd), reach the former site of the **Bald
Hills fire lookout,** on a 2170-m (7117-ft) promontory. The
hitching posts are for the tourist-laden horse trains.

If you stay on the road and pass the optional cutoff trail, you'll
quickly reach a signed junction at 3.2 km (2 mi). Right drops
to Evelyn Creek and intersects the Skyline trail. Bear left,
soon attaining views northeast to the rust-coloured Opal Hills
(Trip 4), and north to where the Jacques Lake trail (Trip 1)
threads between the Colin and Queen Elizabeth ranges.

The road soon levels, looping south then east. About 1½ hours
from the trailhead, at 5.2 km (3.2 mi), reach the lookout site
described above. Follow the road another 70 m (77 yd) to
descend left via the cutoff trail.

To escape mounted tourists and attain a 360° vista, hike higher.
A 20-minute ascent south-southwest gaining 150 m (492 ft) in
1 km (0.6 mi) will grant you the 2320-m (7610-ft) **summit of the
second bald hill,** which is crowned with a big, stoneman cairn.

From the cairn, continue right (southwest) to see Evelyn Creek
valley and the Maligne Range (west). Then turn south and
roam the **ridgecrest** as far as you please.

trip 7

the whistlers /
indian ridge

location	immediately southwest of Jasper townsite
distance	7-km (4.3-mi) round trip to bump #4
	11-km (6.8-mi) ridge circuit
elevation gain	742 m (2434 ft) on round trip to bump #4
	1126 m (3694 ft) on ridge circuit
key elevations	upper gondola terminal 2265 m (7431 ft)
	Whistlers summit 2466 m (8091 ft)
	saddle below summit 2305 m (7562 ft)
	bump #4 on ridge 2685 m (8809 ft)
	ridgecrest highpoint 2715 m (8907 ft)
	basin lowpoint 2200 m (7218 ft)
hiking time	3 ½ to hours for round trip to bump #4
	5 ½ hours for ridge circuit
difficulty	easy to Whistlers summit
	moderate to bump #4
	challenging on circuit
available	late June through early October
map	Gem Trek *Best of Jasper*

opinion

In Jasper townsite, face southwest and look skyward. See the nondescript mountain pierced with towers and strung with cables?

They hoist that gondola up there for good reason: immense scenery. The summit panorama will give your eyeballs an aerobic workout. You can survey all the lakes surrounding the townsite, and a huge chunk of Jasper Park.

On bump #4 of Indian Ridge

But don't hike to the top. Let the gondola whisk you up. You'll gain 960 m (3150 ft) in minutes—an ascent that would take a hardened hiker 2 ½ sweat-drenched hours.

With the time and energy you save, you can spurt past the tourists, ogle the scenery from the Whistlers summit, then dash on, roaming alpine basins and ridges all day.

Though many of the 200,000 people a year who ride the gondola also hike the easy, 1.1-km (0.7-mi) path to the summit, almost none seize the opportunity to explore beyond. You're likely to have the outback to yourself.

Know before you go. Few people are capable of completing the Indian Ridge circuit. You might, however, make it part way up, and even that's a worthwhile accomplishment.

From the Whistlers summit, scope out Indian Ridge (southwest). If what you see makes you hesitant, limit your foray to the basin. But if you're a strong hiker, with some scrambling under your boots, give the ridge a try.

Negotiate the east arm of the ridge first, proceed west along the crest, continue north along the west arm, then return east through the basin. That's all the directional advice you'll need if you're sufficiently experienced to complete the circuit without endangering yourself.

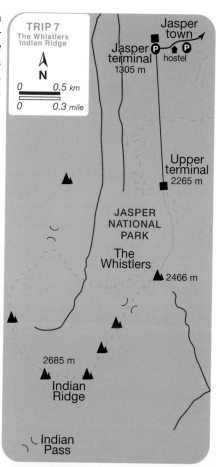

TRIP 7
The Whistlers
Indian Ridge

N

0   0.5 km
0   0.3 mile

Jasper town

Jasper terminal
1305 m

P   P
hostel

Upper terminal
2265 m

JASPER NATIONAL PARK

The Whistlers
▲ 2466 m

2685 m
▲ ▲
Indian Ridge

Indian Pass

The east arm, initially a series of talus-covered bumps, is rugged. There's no trail; only a faint route. Surmounting the ridge highpoint requires a steep traverse, or an exposed spider-walk. A misstep on either could be tragic. So be prepared to turn back, content with whatever triumph is within your comfort zone.

fact

by vehicle

From the junction of Hwy 16 and the Icefields Parkway, at the southwest edge of Jasper townsite, drive the Parkway south 1.8 km (1.1 mi). Turn right

Hardy alpine-zone resident

(west) onto Whistlers Road. Follow it 4 km (2.5 mi) to the large, paved, gondola-base parking lot, at 1305 m (4281 ft).

by gondola

Ride the gondola up to 2265 m (7431 ft). It operates seven days a week. Confirm current schedules and prices with the Jasper Tramway (www.jaspertramway.com, 852-3093 locally, 866-850-8726 toll-free).

on foot

From the upper gondola terminal, climb the boardwalk stairs. Pass the Whistlers trail (right) descending to the base of the mountain. Proceed straight (southwest) on the broad, dirt path.

Gain 201 m (659 ft) in 1.1 km (0.7 mi) to **the Whistlers summit,** marked with a large, stoneman cairn. Elevation: 2466 m (8091 ft). Panorama: 360°.

On a clear day, you'll see all of the following and more. Indian Ridge is nearby southwest, separated from you by a green

South to south-southwest, from Marmot Mountain (Mt. Edith Cavell distant left)

tundra saddle. Marmot Mtn is directly south. Terminal Mtn is just west of south. Manx Peak, shouldering a snowfield, is southwest. In the distance, just north of west, you can identify snow-capped Mt. Robson. The jagged rampart of Mt. Bridgeland is west, in front of Robson. Pyramid Mtn is north. The Colin Range is northeast. The Maligne Range is east.

A path continues beyond The Whistlers summit. It descends, curving northwest. To proceed to Indian Ridge, walk about half way out, then drop left (southwest) into the **saddle.** Bottom-out at 2305 m (7562 ft). Pick up the bootbeaten route, which is now visible, ascending several talus-covered bumps on the east arm of Indian Ridge.

Traverse the northwest side of **bump #1.** Proceed south (left) steeply up **bump #2,** reaching 2535 m (8317 ft). Don't follow the game path right. A fainter route continues to the third, more difficult bump. Stay southeast of the top of **bump #3.** Then scramble straight up (southwest) over 2685-m (8809-ft) **bump #4.** You're now about 1½ hours from the stoneman on the Whistlers summit.

The going is more difficult ahead. Only experienced scramblers should proceed. To reach the base of **bump #5,** cross a short ridge that feels exposed because it's only one m/yd wide. From here, either climb right or traverse left to attain the 2715-m (8907-ft) **crest of Indian Ridge.**

From here on, follow the ridgecrest west, gradually curving north. You need more detailed directions? Whoa. You're in over your head. Turn back.

If you carry on, depart the ridge at 2550 m (8366 ft), where the crest broadens. At that point, the Whistlers summit is almost directly east. Simply work your way down through the basin, then back up to the summit.

options

Prefer rambling to scrambling? From the saddle below the Whistlers summit, descend 105 m (344 ft) west into the verdant basin. From there, ascend northwest to the small saddle on the west arm of Indian Ridge. For a better view, turn left (southwest) and continue ascending Indian Ridge as far as you feel comfortable. Check your watch, so you don't miss the last gondola down.

Interested in a one-way trip? Cross-country trekkers armed with a map and compass can depart the saddle below the Whistlers summit and, heading generally south, skirt Indian Ridge, drop into the Whistlers Creek drainage, climb to Marmot Pass, drop to Portal Creek, intersect the trail, then turn left (northeast) and hike out to Marmot Basin Road. Pre-arrange a shuttle, or rely on your lucky thumb. The trip is doable in a long day.

trip 8

⊗ geraldine lakes

location	south-southwest of Athabasca Falls and the Hwy 93/93-A junction
round trip	10.5 km (6.5 mi) to second lake 13 km (8.1 mi) to fourth lake
elevation gain	407 m (1335 ft) to second lake 497 m (1630 ft) to fourth lake
key elevations	trailhead 1480 m (4854 ft) second lake 1887 m (6190 ft) fourth lake 1976 m (6480 ft)
hiking time	5 hours for second lake 7 hours for fourth lake
difficulty	moderate to second lake challenging to fourth lake
available	early July to late September
map	Gem Trek *Jasper & Maligne Lake*

opinion

When people describe what they enjoy about hiking, they extol the scenic rewards. And that's enough. Witnessing the raw beauty of our unique planet justifies a journey by foot.

But if you keep listening, most will say they hike to experience solitude and tranquility. Probe further and they'll explain how being alone on the trail or mountaintop is comforting, healing, because it restores a measure of balance and sanity to their lives.

Yet there's an even deeper reason most of us hope to be alone beyond the trailhead. It's rarely stated because few are conscious of it, but it's true nonetheless:

The fourth Geraldine Lake

Other people remind us of ourselves, which is precisely what we're out there to lose.

We leave civilization and enter the wilderness to forget ourselves. To meld with something bigger than ourselves. We do it for the same reason we close our eyes when we pray or meditate: to feel we're alone with The Source.

That's why Jasper National Park is immensely appealing to hikers. Less than 5% of park visitors venture onto the 1207 km (750 mi) of trails lacing the 10,878 sq km (4,200 sq mi) of backcountry.

One of Jasper's more secluded dayhikes leads to the Geraldine Lakes, where you'll hike beside streams, past cascades and waterfalls, up a glacier-gouged stairway.

The first of the four Geraldines is pleasant, but forest-ringed, unremarkable, often less than serene. It's a quick, easy hike, suitable for waddlers and toddlers.

Second Geraldine Lake

The second lake is a more worthy goal, a genuine hike requiring strength and tenacity. You'll negotiate a cantankerous trail, roots, rocks, and a steep, wickedly slick ascent. The scenic climax? A plummeting cataract and a tremendous ridgetop vantage.

A little over a kilometer long, the second lake is the biggest of the Geraldines. It's bounded on the east by a rockslide where, if you keep hiking, you'll enjoy continuous views of the lake and nearby mountain walls.

The third and fourth lakes are ethereal sights: pools of deep teal liquid detained in emerald meadows beneath 3360-m (11,024-ft) Mt. Fryatt. But to see these upper lakes you'll have to be tough as a yak.

There's no trail beyond the second lake. The route is discernible thanks to the hardy few who've persisted before you. It requires you to crash through dense brush and krummholz (stunted trees). And it's worth it.

Solitude is likely at the third lake; a near certainty at the fourth. The surrounding alplands are wondrously wild, inviting further exploration. With the courage of Lassie, and a couple extra days, you could enjoy an adventurous cross-country backpack trip here.

Powerful hikers who blast out of the trailhead by 9 a.m. will find the fourth lake a reasonable dayhike destination. Most people will turn around, satisfied, atop the ridge where the second lake is initially visible.

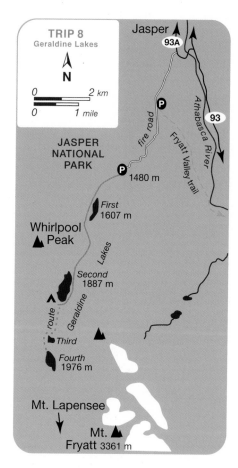

fact

by vehicle

Where Hwy 93-A departs the Icefields Parkway (Hwy 93) at Athabasca Falls (31 km / 19.2 mi south of Jasper townsite), drive 93-A northwest 1.1 km (0.7 mi). Turn left (southwest) onto the narrow, rough, unpaved Geraldine Fire Road. Continue 5.5 km (3.4 mi), switchbacking up through forest, to the trailhead parking lot at 1480 m (4854 ft).

on foot

After a short, mild ascent west, the trail curves left (south) and descends. This will remain your general direction of travel all the way to the fourth lake.

Beneath Whirlpool Peak

Within 20 minutes, reach the forest-shrouded **first lake** at 2 km (1.2 mi), 1607 m (5270 ft). Follow the rough, muddy, rooty path along the west shore for about 15 minutes to the lake's south shore at 2.7 km (1.7 mi).

An hour from the trailhead, approach a 90-m (295-ft) **cascade** and start ascending. Enjoy glimpses of the tumbling water on the way up, because krummholz soon blocks it from view.

The trail climbs over roots and rocks beside the cascade to reach a boulder field. Cairns indicate the way forward. An avalanche slope, draping off a jagged peak, is visible east of the stream. Craggy peaks rise to the west.

Proceed above and left of **shallow tarns**, into a scraggly forest harbouring a confusion of routes. Do not turn west. Continue south, following a path through more rocks.

Begin a steep, 150-m (492-ft) climb left of an impressive **waterfall**. The route is scratched into a rib of dirt and loose rock. Before ascending, be sure you'll be able to safely descend this dicey stretch.

At 5 km (3 mi), crest a **ridge** above the waterfall and attain a broad view. Mt. Fryatt looms southeast. A few minutes farther, the second lake is visible.

Moderate-paced hikers arrive at the north shore of the **second lake** about 2¼ hours after leaving the trailhead. Continue to the far (south) shore by crossing several boulder fields along the east shore.

At 6.2 km (3.8 mi), 1887 m (6190 ft), reach a bridge spanning the second lake's inlet stream. West, just across the bridge, is a small **campground**.

Up for the challenging route to the third and fourth lakes? Don't cross the bridge to the campground. Stay on the east bank. Follow the sketchy, sporadically cairned, bootbeaten path south.

Negotiate a rockslide. After about three cairns, stay right on a narrow, faint track through stunted trees and brush. Wade into thigh-thwacking krummholz for 10 to 15 minutes, then enjoy a respite while crossing more boulders.

Soon depart the creek and march back into krummholz. Visible ahead is an unusually big cairn—a **stoneman**. From there, aim for the lower waterfall at the head of the valley. Beat your way for another five minutes through willow and alder until you're again near the left bank of the creek, where the path resumes in the trees.

Arrive at the **third lake**—smallest of the four, fringed with meadows and krummholz—after 45 minutes of determined hiking from the bridge at the south end of the second lake. To continue, sniff out the path around the right (west) shore of the third lake.

The ramparts of Mt. Fryatt are now more striking. Cross the fourth lake's shallow outlet stream (perhaps on a logjam), scramble up a short, steep rise, and the **fourth lake** is yours. Elevation: 1976 m (6480 ft). Visible south is 3105-m (10,188-ft) Mt. Lapensee. Hiking from outlet to outlet between the upper lakes takes about 25 minutes.

Harebell, or bluebell

It's possible to continue exploring south to a verdurous pass 270 m (885 ft) above and one hour beyond the fourth lake. From there, you can peer down at two lakes that feed Divergence Creek.

trip 9

⊗ verdant pass

location	south of Jasper townsite via Mt. Edith Cavell Road
round trip	23 km (14.3 mi)
elevation gain	665 m (2180 ft) including digressions above and beyond pass
key elevations	trailhead 1730 m (5680 ft) pass 2110 m (6920 ft)
hiking time	7 to 8 hours
difficulty	challenging due only to untracked terrain
available	mid-July to late September
map	Gem Trek *Jasper & Maligne Lake*

opinion

Nature massages your brain. Caressing your cortex with sunshine, kneading your cerebrum with beauty, it softens your stentorian intellect, so you can hear the quiet, pure voice within.

At Verdant Pass, you'll witness nature at its most grand and feral. Hiking here on a fine day is a soothing brain massage that will ensure you give your whispering soul the attention it deserves.

The Verdant Pass meadows are a lavish expanse, bigger than some airports: 2.5 km (1.5 mi) long, 1 km (0.6 mi) wide. Lakes, tarns and creeks shimmer in the green vastness.

The horizon is splashed white by the distant Hooker Icefield. Rampart peaks rise all around, including maelstroms of rock hardened into whirlpool images.

Verdant Pass and the peaks above Whirlpool Valley

Climbers long ago forged this trail up the east side of Verdant Creek valley. Constructed only by the passage of boots, it leads to an ascent route on the back of Mt. Edith Cavell.

The pass is between Edith, which towers above you at neck-craning height, and Chevron Mtn—especially striking when its swirling striations are accentuated by a dusting of snow. Be sure to ascend the hillock guarding Edith's second cirque, where you'll see a teal lake beneath sheer cliffs (see cover photo).

Though seldom used, the narrow, rooty trail is easy to follow. The ascent is initially moderate, but steepens during the final rough stretch to Edith's first cirque. Beyond, there's no trail, so you'll continue exploring cross-country. But because you're above treeline, navigation is easy—if you remain alert.

Still, bring a topo map and compass. None of this trip, even the portion on trail, can you walk absentmindedly. Be especially

Trekking past Chevron Mountain

attentive crossing the meadows, so you don't kerplunk into a bog, wrench an ankle in the tussocks, or become disoriented.

You're in virgin alplands here. Please leave no trace of your passage. Preserve the unsullied majesty of Verdant Pass by hiking abreast of your companions. Single file causes more damage. Wherever possible, walk on rock. Even stepping on hard tussocks is better than on the fragile alpine flora.

fact

by vehicle

From the junction of Hwy 16 and the Icefields Parkway, at the southwest edge of Jasper townsite, drive the Parkway south 7.2 km (4.5 mi). Turn right (west) onto Hwy 93A and follow it south 5.3 km (3.3 mi). Turn right onto Mount Edith Cavell Road and follow it 12.2 km (7.6 mi) to the Tonquin Valley (Astoria River) trailhead parking area, just past the youth hostel. Elevation: 1730 m (5680 ft).

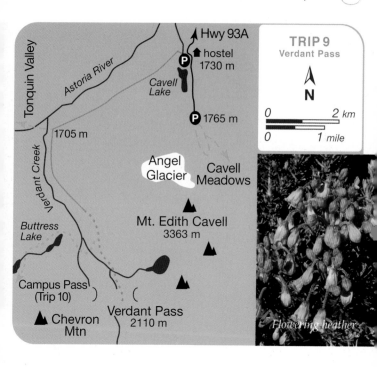

TRIP 9
Verdant Pass

Tonquin Valley

Astoria River

Hwy 93A

hostel
1730 m

Cavell
Lake

1765 m

1705 m

Verdant Creek

Angel
Glacier

Cavell
Meadows

Mt. Edith Cavell
3363 m

Buttress
Lake

Campus Pass
(Trip 10)

Chevron
Mtn

Verdant Pass
2110 m

Flowering heather

0   2 km
0   1 mile

on foot

From the north end of the parking area, descend the old dirt road. Cross the bridge spanning the Cavell Lake outlet stream. Go up the hill and turn right to avoid a horse corral.

You're now on the **Astoria River trail,** gradually descending southwest. This is the expressway to Tonquin Valley. The broad, smooth path allows fast striding.

After hiking 4.5 km (2.8 mi) in about one hour, turn left (south) onto the narrow, unsigned, **Verdant Pass trail** at 1705 m (5592 ft). Opposite this fork is a flat, 1.5-m (5-ft) long boulder on the right.

From here, the Astoria River trail continues descending. If you miss the Verdant Pass trail, in 0.4 km (0.25 mi) you'll reach a wood bridge spanning Verdant Creek. Turn back.

Southwest face of Mount Edith Cavell

The narrow, rooty trail to Verdant Pass ascends moderately through forest. After gaining 158 m (520 ft) from the junction, a level stretch grants you a respite.

Soon, about 7.5 km (4.7 mi) from the trailhead, the path deteriorates, climbing steeply into subalpine meadows. Below (right / west) is a deep gorge. Angle left, up the lower slopes of Mt. Edith Cavell.

Follow the dwindling path across a creeklet, then over the top of a gentle rise at the mouth of **Edith's first cirque.** You're near 8.5 km (5.3 mi) and just above 2200 m (7200 ft), having gained 500 m (1640 ft) from the Astoria River trail.

A sketchy route continues left (east) into the first cirque. It dead-ends in talus, above a tiny tarn. Ignore it. Verdant Pass is visible below you, south. Edith's second cirque is southeast.

From this point on, you're exploring cross-country, choosing your own route. Stay aware of the terrain, so you can find your way back. The following guidelines might help.

Head southeast across the heather. Descend 15 m/yd down a rockslide. Continue along the bottom edge of the rocks for a few minutes, to a green basin. As you approach a large tarn, there's a heathery hillock on your left (east), at the mouth of **Edith's second cirque.**

You're now on the north edge of Verdant Pass. The northeast-facing crags of 2879-m (9446-ft) Chevron Mtn are west, across the creek drainage. The Hooker Icefield is visible south.

Before proceeding into the pass, scramble 50 m (160 ft) up the hillock to see the teal lake beneath sheer cliffs. Afterward, descend the hillock by veering left toward the smaller tarn and creeklet in the green basin below. Reach **Verdant Pass** at 11.5 km (7.1 mi), 2110 m (6920 ft).

Proceeding deeper into the pass, weave through stunted trees and cross tussocky meadowland. Descending the south side of the pass, angle right (southwest) to stay on the edge of a meandering stream and boggy meadows. A boulder field provides the easiest and most eco-sensitive route.

The Whirlpool peaks are obvious, southeast. A grassy ridge southwest is the optimal vantage and logical turnaround point for a dayhike. From there, you can survey the Whirlpool River valley, and the Divergence Creek valley between Mt. Lapensee (left / northeast) and Divergence Peak (right / southwest).

trip 10

campus pass

location	south of Jasper townsite via Mt. Edith Cavell Road
round trip	32 km (19.8 mi)
elevation gain	968 m (3175 ft)
key elevations	trailhead 1730 m (5680 ft) Buttress Lake 2035 m (6677 ft) Campus Pass 2270 m (7448 ft)
hiking time	10 to 12 hours
difficulty	challenging
available	mid-July through mid-September
map	Gem Trek *Jasper & Maligne Lake*

opinion

"The *adventure* begins here!"

"*Discover* the possibilities!"

"A world of wonders for you to *explore*!"

Marketing hype has debased many of our most potent words. They're now clichés—the linguistic equivalent of clowns—humiliated by advertising hacks who've misused them to describe amusement parks, shopping malls, and real-estate developments.

"Adventure," "discovery," and "exploration" are vital nouns endowed with distinct meaning. Using them in reference to Ernest Shackleton, Neil Armstrong, or Reinhold Messner is justified. But suggesting they accurately portray the Campus Pass trip—even though it's a rigourous endeavour—would be an exaggeration.

Throne Mountain, from below Verdant Pass

Knowing that we fully respect those gallant words, however, and that they sprang to mind when writing this description, will help you imagine the trip you've begun reading about.

Attempting the Campus Pass circuit in a single day is ambitious. Unless you're a strong hiker, experienced at cross-country navigation, comfortable on trail-less terrain, willing to crash through bush, capable on steep slopes, knowledgeable about bear safety, and equipped to bivouac should something go awry, postpone this trip.

You're equal to the challenge? Lucky you. Completing the circuit is a triumph. The scenery is electroconvulsive. This will likely rank among your hiking career's sweetest accomplishments and most vivid memories.

Read about Verdant Pass (Trip 9). That's just the first leg of the Campus Pass circuit. After overlooking Verdant Pass, you'll turn away, cross an arm of Chevron Mtn, drop to Buttress Lake, pass Beryl Lake, enter a virgin basin, vault over Campus Pass, traverse the torso of Blackhorn Peak, then careen back into the Astoria River valley where you'll probably unleash a conquistadorial yell upon intersecting a trail for the final, easy, victory lap.

The journey is a visual feast. But the section from Campus Pass around to the north side of Blackhorn Peak is dessert. The crème brûlée of the day. Slow your pace here. Stop often. Savour it. You'll see the sprawling alplands of Campus Creek basin, the towering Ramparts, and the Amethyst Lakes in Tonquin Valley—all from an astonishing aerial perspective.

Later, should you voice the opinion that the view of Tonquin from Blackhorn is the most spectacular in Jasper Park, no one—not even the most experienced backcountry warden— would debate you.

Wait until midsummer to attempt the Campus Pass circuit. Pick a day when you have a signed certificate in hand guaranteeing perfect weather. Start the trip early—earlier than you'd prefer— so you'll have time to correct any navigational errors and still enjoy the entire hike without feeling pressured by twilight.

Bring a topo map and compass. (You do know how to use them, right?) Wear long pants and a longsleeve shirt, for grappling with krummholz. Start hydrated, pack a couple liters of water person person, refill at every opportunity. Carry several more energy bars than you think you'll need. And make noise frequently to warn bears of your approach.

Buttress Lake (Trip 10)

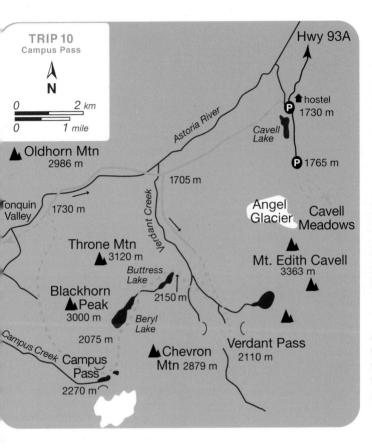

fact

by vehicle

From the junction of Hwy 16 and the Icefields Parkway, at the southwest edge of Jasper townsite, drive the Parkway south 7.2 km (4.5 mi). Turn right (west) onto Hwy 93A and follow it south 5.3 km (3.3 mi). Turn right onto Mount Edith Cavell Road and follow it 12.2 km (7.6 mi) to the Tonquin Valley (Astoria River) trailhead parking area, just past the youth hostel. Elevation: 1730 m (5680 ft).

Alpine meadows northwest of Campus Pass

on foot

From the north end of the parking area, descend the old dirt road. Cross the bridge spanning the Cavell Lake outlet stream. Go up the hill and turn right to avoid a horse corral.

You're now on the **Astoria River trail,** gradually descending southwest. This is the expressway to Tonquin Valley. The broad, smooth path allows fast striding.

After hiking 4.5 km (2.8 mi) in about one hour, turn left (south) onto the narrow, unsigned, **Verdant Pass trail** at 1705 m (5592 ft). Opposite this fork is a flat, 1.5-m (5-ft) long boulder on the right.

From here, the Astoria River trail continues descending. If you miss the Verdant Pass trail, in 0.4 km (0.25 mi) you'll reach a wood bridge spanning Verdant Creek. Turn back.

The narrow, rooty trail to Verdant Pass ascends moderately through forest. After gaining 158 m (520 ft) from the junction, a level stretch grants you a respite.

Soon, about 7.5 km (4.7 mi) from the trailhead, the path deteriorates, climbing steeply into subalpine meadows. Below (right / west) is a deep gorge. Angle left, up the lower slopes of Mt. Edith Cavell.

Follow the dwindling path across a creeklet, then over the top of a gentle rise at the mouth of **Edith's first cirque.** You're near 8.5 km (5.3 mi) and just above 2200 m (7200 ft), having gained 500 m (1640 ft) from the Astoria River trail.

A sketchy route continues left (east) into the first cirque. It dead-ends in talus, above a tiny tarn. Ignore it. **Verdant Pass** is visible below you, south, at 2110 m (6920 ft). Edith's second cirque is southeast.

From this point on, you're navigating cross-country, choosing your own route. Stay aware of the terrain, so you can find your way back should you abort the trip. The following suggestions might aid your progress.

Your immediate goal is the ridgecrest east of Buttress Lake's north shore. It's actually the north-northeast arm of Chevron Mountain. Though it's directly west of where you are now (at the mouth of Edith's first cirque), a contouring, looping approach will spare you significant bushwhacking and elevation loss.

In general, head south-southwest. Drop no lower than about 2100 m (6890 ft). Rockhop the two **upper forks of Verdant Creek.** Then veer north, ascending gradually, seeking the path of least resistance.

Crest the **ridge above Buttress Lake** at about 11.5 km (7.1 mi), 2150 m (7054 ft). The lake is visible below (west). Your next assignment: descend the steep slope to the north shore. You must bash your way through thick krummholz, but at least it prevents you from falling.

Upon reaching **Buttress Lake** at 2035 m (6677 ft), round the north shore, then head southwest above the west shore. You'll encounter more krummholz, but it ends soon.

Approaching **Beryl Lake,** rockhop the outlet stream, then continue boulder-hopping south-southwest along the east shore at 2075 m (6808 ft).

Pass Beryl's south shore and begin ascending to Campus Pass, which is visible ahead (south). Cascading streamlets grace the headwall basin. The meadowy slope allows easy travel.

Surmount 2270-m (7448-ft) **Campus Pass** at about 16 km (9.9 mi). The new view west encompasses a sweeping expanse of gentle alplands.

You're overlooking **Campus Creek basin.** The mountains forming the basin's southwest wall are unnamed. Tarns in the pass feed the creek, which flows east, then north into the Astoria River.

After a well-earned idyll, descend west maybe 50 m (164 ft), then begin contouring northwest at about 2200 m (7218 ft), across the heathery southwest slope of 3000-m (9840-ft) **Blackhorn Peak.** Don't drift downward. Stay high.

The famous Tonquin Valley—where The Ramparts rise abruptly from the Amethyst Lakes—is increasingly visible as you travel northwest.

After maintaining your elevation, ascend slightly, pierce a scrim of krummholz, and begin curving right (northeast) around Blackhorn Peak. Stay above treeline as long as possible.

Continue until you see the **ravine** that cleaves Blackhorn Peak and Throne Mtn. Here, on Blackhorn's north slope, you've reached the end of easy alpine rambling. Total distance so far: about 21 km (13 mi).

Turn left (north-northwest) and begin a lengthy, steep descent, following the **unnamed creek** but staying comfortably above its southwest bank. Only initially can you avoid the trees. You'll soon be bush-bashing downslope: a 50-minute chore that might feel longer. At least you're not fighting gravity too.

Keep the creek within earshot if not within sight. It's your temporary guide. Just keep following it down until you intersect

The Ramparts and Amethyst Lakes, from Campus Pass

the trail linking Chrome Lake and the Wates-Gibson Hut (left/ west) with the Astoria River campground (right/northeast).

Upon reaching the **trail** at 1730 m (5676 ft), you'll have hiked about 22.5 km (14 mi). Shake the twigs from your hair, empty the detritus from your boots, let out a victory whoop, turn right and hike northeast, happy in the knowledge that it's easy striding from here on.

Cross a bridge spanning the **Astoria River** at 23.7 km (14.7 mi). On the north bank, intersect the broader, more comfortable Astoria River trail. Bear right (east-northeast).

Pass the Astoria River campground at 25.1 km (15.6 mi). Proceed east. Cross a bridge back to the river's south bank at 26.6 km (16.5 mi).

After a short ascent, cross the bridge over Verdant Creek, then pass the unsigned **Verdant Pass trail** (right/south). You've completed the circuit and are now on familiar ground.

Continue the gradual ascent northeast on the Astoria River trail. Reach the trailhead **parking area** at 32 km (19.8 mi).

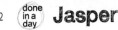
PREPARE FOR YOUR HIKE

Hiking in the Canadian Rockies is an adventure. Adventure involves risk. But the rewards are worth it. Just be ready for more adventure than you expect.

The weather here is constantly changing. Even on a warm, sunny day, pack for rain or snow. Injury is always a possibility. On a long dayhike, be equipped to spend the night out.

If you respect the power of wilderness by being prepared, you'll decrease the risk, increase your comfort and enjoyment, and come away fulfilled, yearning for more.

You Carry What You Are

Even with all the right gear, you're ill-equipped without physical fitness.

If the weather turns grim, the physical capability to escape the wilderness fast might keep you from being stuck in a life-threatening situation. If you're fit, and a companion gets injured, you can race for help.

Besides, if you're not overweight or easily exhausted, you'll have more fun. You'll be able to hike farther, reach more spectacular scenery, and leave crowds behind.

So if you're out of shape, work on it. Everything else you'll need is easier to acquire.

Travel Light

Weight is critical when hiking, especially when backpacking. But even when dayhiking, the lighter you travel, the easier and more pleasant the journey.

Some people are mules; they can shoulder everything they might conceivably want. If you'd rather be a thoroughbred, reduce your burden by getting lighter gear and packing it with discretion.

Be prepared for a sudden weather change, even when dayhiking.

You might have to sacrifice a few luxuries to be more agile, fleet-footed and comfortable on the trail—your bulky fleece jacket, for example, or an apple each for your spouse and three kids—but you'll be a happier hiker.

Lighter boots, clothing and packs are more expensive because the materials are finer, the engineering smarter, and the craftsmanship superior. But they're worth it. Consult reputable outdoor stores for specific brands.

Layer with Synthetics

Don't just wear a T-shirt and throw a heavy sweatshirt in your pack. Cotton kills. It quickly gets saturated with perspiration and takes way too long to dry. Wet clothing saps your body heat and could lead to hypothermia, a leading cause of death in the outdoors.

Your mountain clothes should be made of fabrics that wick sweat away from your skin, insulate when wet, and dry rapidly. Merino superfine wool, or synthetics like Capilene are ideal. Even your hiking shorts and underwear should be at least partly synthetic. Sports bras should be entirely synthetic.

There are now lots of alternatives to the soggy T-shirt. All outdoor clothing companies offer shortsleeve shirts in superior, synthetic versions. Unlike cotton T-shirts, sweat-soaked synthetics can dry during a rest break.

For warmth, several synthetic layers are more efficient than a single parka. Your body temperature varies constantly on the trail, in response to the weather and your activity level. With only one warm garment, it's either on or off, roast or freeze. Layers allow you to fine tune for optimal comfort.

In addition to a synthetic shortsleeve shirt, it's smart to pack two longsleeve tops (zip-T's) of different fabric weights: one thin, one thick. Wear the thin one for cool-weather hiking. It'll be damp when you stop for a break, so change into the thick one. When you start again, put the thin one back on.

The idea is to always keep your thick top dry in case you really need it to stay warm. Covered by a rain shell (jacket), these two tops can provide enough warmth on summer dayhikes. You can always wear your shortsleeve shirt like a vest over a longsleeve top.

For more warmth while hiking, try a fleece vest. For more warmth at rest stops, consider a down vest or down sweater. But don't hike in down clothing; it'll get sweat soaked and become useless.

For your legs, bring a pair of tights or long underwear. Choose tights made of synthetic insulating material, with a small percentage of lycra for stretch mobility. These are warmer and more durable than the all-lycra or nylon/lycra tights runners wear.

Tights are generally more efficient than pants. They stretch, conforming to your movement. They're lighter and insulate better. You can wear them for hours in a drizzle and not feel damp.

If you're too modest to sport this sleek look, bring ultra-light long underwear you can slip on beneath light hiking pants—a combination that's also more wind resistant than tights.

The right mountain clothing will enhance your comfort, performance and safety.

Anticipating hot weather? Bugs? Intense sun? You'll want long pants and a long-sleeve shirt, both made of tightly-woven synthetics and as lightweight as possible.

Though resembling a dress shirt or blouse—collar, button front, cuffs—your hiking shirt should be designed specifically for vigourous activity. Most outdoor clothing manufacturers offer them.

Your hiking pants should have a loose, unrestrictive fit. You can lift a knee above your hips without pulling the waistband down your butt? Perfect.

Raingear

Pack a full set of raingear: shell and pants. The shell (jacket) should have a hood. Fabrics that are both waterproof and breathable are best, because they repel rain and vent perspiration vapour. Gore-tex has long been the fabric of choice, but there are now many alternatives—equally effective, yet less expensive.

Don't let a blue sky or promising weather forecast tempt you to leave your raingear behind. It can be invaluable, even if you don't encounter rain. Worn over insulating layers, a shell and pants will shed wind, retain body heat, and keep you much warmer.

Coated-nylon raingear appears to be a bargain solution, but it doesn't breathe, so it simulates a steam bath if worn while exercising. You'll end up as damp from sweat as you would from rain.

Lacking technical raingear, you're better off with a poncho. On a blustery day, a poncho won't provide impervious protection from rain, but it allows enough air circulation so you won't get sweat soaked.

Boots and Socks

Lightweight fabric boots with even a little ankle support are more stable and safer than runners. But all-leather or highly technical leather/fabric boots offer superior comfort and performance. For serious hiking, they're a necessity.

If it's a rugged, quality boot, a light- or medium-weight pair should be adequate for most hiking conditions. Heavy boots will slow you down, just like an overweight pack. But you want boots with hard, protective toes, or you'll risk a broken or sprained digit.

Lateral support stops ankle injuries. Stiff shanks keep your feet from tiring. Grippy outsoles prevent slipping and falling. And sufficient cushioning lessens the pain of a long day on the trail.

Out of the box, boots should be waterproof or at least very water resistant, although you'll have to treat them often to maintain their repellency. Boots with lots of seams allow water to seep in as they age. A full rand (wraparound bumper) adds an extra measure of water protection.

The key consideration is comfort. Make sure your boots don't hurt. If you wait to find out until after a day of hiking, it's too late; you're stuck with them. So before purchasing, ask the retailer if, after wearing them indoors, you can exchange them if they don't feel right. A half-hour of walking in a hotel or mall is a helpful test.

Socks are important too. To keep your feet dry, warm and happy, wear wool, thick acrylic, or wool/acrylic-blend socks.

Cotton socks retain sweat, cause blisters, and are especially bad if your boots aren't waterproof. It's usually best to wear two pairs of socks, with a thinner, synthetic pair next to your feet to wick away moisture and alleviate friction, minimizing the chance of blisters.

Gloves and Hats

Always bring gloves and a hat. You've probably heard it, and it's true: your body loses most of its heat through your head and extremities. Cover them if you get chilled. Carry thin, synthetic gloves to wear while hiking. Don't worry if they get wet, but keep a pair of thicker fleece gloves dry in your pack. A fleece hat, or at least a thick headband that covers your ears, adds a lot of warmth and weighs little. A hat with a long brim is essential to shade your eyes and protect your face from sun exposure.

Trekking Poles

Long, steep ascents and descents in the Canadian Rockies make

trekking poles vital. Hiking with poles is easier, more enjoyable, and less punishing to your body. If you're constantly pounding the trails, they could add years to your mountain life.

Working on a previous guidebook, we once hiked for a month without poles. Both of us developed knee pain.

Using trekking poles is like shifting into 4WD. Plus, by alleviating stress to your body they can add years to your mountain life.

The next summer we used Leki trekking poles every day for three months and our knees were never strained. We felt like four-legged animals. We were more surefooted. Our speed and endurance increased.

Studies show that during a typical eight-hour hike you'll transfer more than 250 tons of pressure to a pair of trekking poles. When going downhill, poles significantly reduce stress to your knees, as well as your ankles and lower back.

They alleviate knee strain when you're going uphill too, because you're climbing with your arms and shoulders, not just your legs. Poles also improve your posture. They keep you more upright, which gives you greater lung capacity and allows more efficient breathing.

Regardless how light you daypack is, you'll appreciate the support of trekking poles. They're especially helpful for crossing unbridged streams, traversing steep slopes, and negotiating muddy, rooty, rough stretches of trail.

Poles prevent ankle sprains—a common hiking injury. By making you more stable, they actually help you relax, boosting your sense of security and confidence.

Don't carry one of those big, heavy, gnarled, wooden staffs, unless you're going to a costume party dressed as Gandalf. They're more burden than benefit.

A pair of old ski poles will suffice. They're not as effective or comfortable as poles designed specifically for trekking, but they're better than hiking empty handed.

If possible, invest in a pair of true trekking poles with a soft anti-shock system and adjustable, telescoping, super-lock shafts. We strongly recommend Leki.

First Aid

Someone in your hiking party should carry a first-aid kit. Prepackaged kits look handy, but they're expensive, and some are inadequate. If you make your own, you'll be more familiar with the contents.

Include an antibacterial ointment; pain pills with ibuprofen, and a few with codeine for agonizing injuries; regular bandages; several sizes of butterfly bandages; a couple bandages big enough to hold a serious laceration together; rolls of sterile gauze and absorbent pads to staunch bleeding; adhesive tape; tiny fold-up scissors or a small knife; and a compact first-aid manual.

Duct tape can help prevent blisters.

Whether your kit is store bought or homemade, check the expiration dates on your medications every year and replace them as needed.

Instead of the old elastic bandages for wrapping sprains, we now carry neoprene ankle and knee bands. They slip on instantly, require no special wrapping technique, keep the injured joint warmer, and stay in place better. They're so convenient, you can quickly slip them on for extra support on long, steep, rough descents.

Bandanas

A bandana will be the most versatile item in your pack. Carry at least two when dayhiking.

You can use a bandana to blow your nose, mop your brow, or improvise a beanie. It makes a colourful headband that will keep sweat or hair out of your eyes. It serves as a bandage or sling in a medical emergency.

Worn as a neckerchief, a bandana prevents a sunburned neck. If you soak it in water, then drape it around your neck, it will help keep you from overheating.

Worn Lawrence-of-Arabia style under a hat, a bandana shades both sides of your face, as well as your neck, while deterring mosquitoes. For an air-conditioning effect, soak it in water then don it á la Lawrence.

When shooing away bugs, flicking a bandana with your wrist is less tiresome than flailing your arms.

Small and Essential

A closed-cell foam pad, just big enough to sit on, weighs little but makes rest breaks more comfortable and therefore restful. If an emergency ever forces you to spend a night out, having a foam pad might be the difference between a tolerable experience and a miserable one.

In a crisis, it might be necessary to start a fire to keep warm. Carry matches in a plastic bag, so they'll stay dry. It's wise to have a lighter, too. Finger-size fire starters (Optimus Firelighter or Coghlan FireSticks) are a godsend in wet weather.

Pack an emergency survival bag. One fits into the palm of your hand and could help you survive a cold night without a sleeping bag or tent. The ultralight, metallic fabric reflects your body heat back at you. Survival bags, which you crawl into, are more efficient than survival blankets.

Bring plastic bags in various sizes. Use the small ones for packing whatever garbage you generate or find. A couple large trash bags could be used to improvise a shelter.

A headlamp is often helpful and can be necessary for safety. You'll need one to stay on the trail if you're forced to hike after sunset. Carry spare batteries.

Most people find mosquito repellent indispensable. If you anticipate an infestation, bring a head net made of fine, nylon mesh.

For those dreaded blisters, pack Moleskin or Spenco gel. Cut it with the knife or scissors you should have in your first-aid kit.

Wind and glare will quickly strain your eyes and might give you a headache. Sun exposure can cause cataracts and cancer. Wear sunglasses, a hat with a brim, and sunscreen.

Remember to stuff your brain with provocative questions to ask your companions. Hiking stimulates meaningful conversation.

Keep It All Dry

Most packs are not waterproof, or even very water resistant. To protect your gear from rain, put it in plastic bags and use a waterproof pack cover. Rain is a constant likelihood, so you might as well start hiking with everything in bags. That's easier than wrestling with it in a storm. For added assurance, light-weight, waterproof stuffsacks are superior to plastic bags.

Water

Drink water frequently. Keeping your body hydrated is essential. If you're thirsty, you're probably not performing at optimal efficiency.

But be aware of giardia lamblia, a waterborne parasitic cyst that causes severe gastrointestinal distress. It's transported through animal and human feces, so never defecate or urinate near water.

To be safe, assume giardia is present in all surface water in the Canadian Rockies. Don't drink any water unless it's directly from a source you're certain is pure, like meltwater dripping off glacial ice, or until you've disinfected or filtered it.

Killing giardia by disinfecting it with iodine tablets can be tricky. The colder the water,

Purifying water

done
in a
day

the longer you must wait. Iodine also makes the water smell and taste awful, unless you use neutralizing pills. And iodine has no effect whatsoever on cryptosporidium, an increasingly common cyst that causes physical symptoms identical to giardiasis.

Carrying a small, lightweight filter is a reasonable solution. Some filters weigh just 240 grams (8 ounces). To strain out giardia cysts, your filter must have an absolute pore size of 4 microns or less. Straining out cryptosporidium cysts requires an absolute pore size of 2 microns or less.

After relying on water filters for many years, we've switched to Pristine water purification droplets (www.pristine.ca). The active ingredient is chlorine dioxide, which has been used for more than 50 years in hundreds of water treatment plants throughout North America and Europe.

The Pristine system comprises two 30-ml bottles with a total combined weight of only 80 grams (2.8 ounces). It purifies up to 120 liters (30 gallons) of water. Using it is simple: mix two solutions, wait five minutes, then add it to your water. You can drink 15 minutes later knowing you won't contract giardia. Treating for cryptosporidium requires a higher dosage and/or longer wait.

Body Fuel

When planning meals, keep energy and nutrition foremost in mind. During a six-hour hike, you'll burn 1800 to 3000 calories, depending on terrain, pace, body size, and pack weight. You'll be stronger, and therefore safer and happier, if you tank up on high-octane body fuel.

A white-flour bun with a thick slab of meat or cheese on it is low-octane fuel. Too much protein or fat will make you feel sluggish and drag you down. And you won't get very far up the trail snacking on candy bars. Refined sugars give you a brief spurt that quickly fizzles.

For sustained exercise, like hiking, you need protein and fat to function normally and give you that satisfying full feeling. The speed of your metabolism determines how much protein and fat you should eat. Both are hard to digest. Your body takes three or four hours to assimilate them, compared to one or two hours for carbohydrates.

That's why a carb-heavy diet is optimal for hiking. It ensures your blood supply keeps hustling oxygen to your legs, instead of diverted it to your stomach. Most people, however, can sustain athletic effort longer if their carb-heavy diet includes a little protein. So eat a small portion of protein in the morning, a smaller portion at lunch, and a moderate portion at dinner to aid muscle repair.

For athletic performance, the American and Canadian Dietetic Association recommends that 60 to 65% of your total energy come from carbs, less than 25% from fat, and 15% from protein. They also say refined carbs and sugars should account for no more than 10% of your total carb calories.

Toiling muscles crave the glycogen your body manufactures from complex carbs. Yet your body has limited carb storage capacity. So your carb intake should be constant. That means loading your pack with plant foods made of whole-grain flour, rice, corn, oats, legumes, nuts, seeds, fruit and vegetables.

Dining Out

Natural- or health-food stores are reliable sources of hiking food. They even stock energy bars, which are superior to candy bars because they contain more carbs and less fat.

Always bring a few more energy bars than you think you'll need. We rely on Power Bars. They energize us faster and sustain us longer than any brand we've tried.

For lunch, how about a whole-grain pita pocket filled with tabouli, hummus, avocado, cucumbers and sprouts?

Lyall's saxifrage

Another favourite of ours is marinated tofu that's been pressed, baked, and vacuum-packed. It's protein rich, delicious, and lasts unrefrigerated for more than a day.

Omnivores have other excellent protein options: hard-boiled eggs, free-range bison jerky, and vacuum-packed wild salmon in tear-open bags. Eat cheese sparingly; beyond small amounts, it's unhealthy.

In addition to our main course, we usually bring a bag of organic tortilla chips (corn or mixed-grain) cooked in expeller-pressed safflower or canola oil.

For snacks, carry dried fruit; whole-grain cookies made with natural sweeteners (brown-rice syrup, organic cane-sugar, fruit juice, raw honey); or whole-grain crackers.

INFORMATION SOURCES

Dwarf saw-wort

Jasper National Park
www.pc.gc.ca/jasper

Jasper Tourism
www.jaspercanadianrockies.com

Jasper Home Accommodation
www.stayinjasper.com
PO Box 758, Jasper, AB, T0E 1E0
jtc@stayinjasper.com

Hostelling International
www.hihostels.ca
(780) 852-3215, 1-877-852-0781

Weather
www.theweathernetwork.com

INDEX

THE AUTHORS

Kathy and Craig are dedicated to each other, and to hiking, in that order. Their second date was a 32-km (20-mile) dayhike in Arizona. Since then they haven't stopped for long.

They've trekked through much of the world's vertical topography, including the Himalayas, Patagonian Andes, Spanish Pyrenees, Swiss Alps, Scottish Highlands, Italian Dolomites, and New Zealand Alps. In North America, they've explored the B.C. Coast, Selkirk and Purcell ranges, Montana's Beartooth Wilderness, Wyoming's Grand Tetons, the California Sierra, Washington's North Cascades, and the Colorado Rockies.

In 1989 they moved from the U.S. to Canada, so they could live near the Canadian Rockies—the range that inspired the first of their refreshingly unconventional guidebooks: *Don't Waste Your Time in the Canadian Rockies, The Opinionated Hiking Guide.* Its popularity encouraged them to abandon their careers— Kathy as an ESL teacher, Craig as an ad-agency creative director—and start their own guidebook publishing company: hikingcamping.com.

Though the distances they hike are epic, Kathy and Craig agree that hiking, no matter how far, is the easiest of the many tasks necessary to create a guidebook. What they find most challenging is having to sit at their Canmore, Alberta, home, with the Canadian Rockies visible out the window. But they do it every winter, spending twice as much time at their computers—writing, organizing, editing, checking facts—as they do on the trail.

The result is worth it. Kathy and Craig's colourful writing, opinionated commentary, and enthusiasm for the joys of hiking make their guidebooks uniquely helpful and compelling.

Other Titles from hikingcamping.com

The following titles—boot-tested and written by the Opinionated Hikers, Kathy & Craig Copeland—are widely available in outdoor shops and bookstores. Visit www.hikingcamping.com to read excerpts and purchase online. The website also offers updates for each book, recent reports on trails and campsites, and details about new titles such as the *Done in a Day* series.

Don't Waste Your Time in the Canadian Rockies®
The Opinionated Hiking Guide

ISBN 0-9689419-7-4 Even here, in a mountain range designated a UNESCO World Heritage Site for its "superlative natural phenomena" and "exceptional natural beauty and aesthetic importance," not all scenery is equal. Some destinations are simply more striking, more intriguing, more inspiring than others. Now you can be certain you're choosing a rewarding hike for your weekend or vacation. This uniquely helpful, visually captivating guidebook covers Banff, Jasper, Kootenay, Yoho and Waterton Lakes national parks, plus Mt. Robson and Mt. Assiniboine provincial parks. It rates each trail *Premier, Outstanding, Worthwhile,* or *Don't Do,* explains why, and provides comprehensive route descriptions. 138 dayhikes and backpack trips. Trail maps for each hike. 544 pages, 270 photos, full colour throughout. 5th edition updated July 2006.

Where Locals Hike
in the Canadian Rockies
The Premier Trails in Kananaskis
Country, near Canmore and Calgary

ISBN 978-0-9783427-4-6 The 55 most
rewarding dayhikes and backpack
trips within two hours of Calgary's
international airport. All lead to
astonishing alpine meadows, ridges
and peaks. Though these trails are
little known compared to those in the
nearby Canadian Rocky Mountain
national parks, the scenery is equally
magnificent. Includes Peter Lougheed
and Spray Valley provincial parks. Discerning trail reviews
help you choose your trip. Detailed route descriptions keep
you on the path. 320 pages, 180 photos, trail maps for each
hike, full colour throughout. Updated 3rd edition August 2008.

Where Locals Hike
in the West Kootenay
The Premier Trails in Southeast B.C.
near Kaslo & Nelson

ISBN 978-0-9689419-9-7 See the
peaks, glaciers and cascades that
make locals passionate about these
mountains. The 50 most rewarding
dayhikes and backpack trips in the
Selkirk and west Purcell ranges of
southeast British Columbia. Includes
Valhalla, Kokanee Glacier, and
Goat Range parks, as well as hikes near Arrow, Slocan, and
Kootenay lakes. Discerning trail reviews help you choose your
trip. Detailed route descriptions keep you on the path. 272
pages, 130 photos, trail locator maps, full colour throughout.
Updated 2nd edition April 2007.

Camp Free in B.C.

ISBN 978-0-9735099-3-9 Make your weekend or vacation adventurous and revitalizing. Enjoy British Columbia's scenic byways and 2WD backroads—in your low-clearance car or your big RV. Follow precise directions to 350 campgrounds, from the B.C. Coast to the Rocky Mountains. Choose from 80 low-fee campgrounds similar in quality to provincial parks but half the price. Find retreats where the world is

yours alone. Simplify life: slow down, ease up. Fully appreciate B.C.'s magnificent backcountry, including the Sunshine Coast, Okanagan, Shuswap Highlands, Selkirk and Purcell ranges, Cariboo Mountains, and Chilcotin Plateau. 544 pages, 200 photos, 20 regional maps, full colour throughout. Updated 4th edition April 2007.

Gotta Camp Alberta

ISBN 978-0-9735099-0-8 Make your weekend or vacation adventurous and revitalizing. Enjoy Alberta's scenic byways and 2WD backroads— in your low-clearance car or your big RV. Follow precise directions to 150 idyllic campgrounds, from the foothill lakes to the Rocky Mountains. Camp in national parks, provincial parks, and recreation areas. Find retreats where the world is yours alone. Simplify life: slow down, ease up.

Return home soothed by the serenity of nature. Approximately 400 pages, 170 photos, and 18 maps. Full colour throughout. First edition June 2008.

Hiking from Here to WOW: North Cascades
50 Trails to the Wonder of Wilderness

ISBN 978-0-89997-444-6 The authors hiked more than 1,400 miles through North Cascades National Park plus the surrounding wilderness areas, including Glacier Peak, Mt. Baker, and the Pasayten. They took more than 1,000 photos and hundreds of pages of field notes. Then they culled their list of favourite hikes down to 50 trips—each selected for its power to incite awe. Their 264-page book describes where to find the cathedral forests, psychedelic meadows, spiky summits, and colossal glaciers that distinguish the American Alps. And it does so in refreshing style: honest, literate, entertaining, inspiring. Like all *WOW Guides*, this one is full colour throughout, with 180 photos and a trail map for each dayhike and backpack trip. First edition May 2007.

Hiking from Here to WOW: Utah Canyon Country
95 Trails to the Wonder of Wilderness

ISBN 978-0-89997-452-1 The authors hiked more than 1,600 miles through Zion, Bryce, Escalante-Grand Staircase, Glen Canyon, Grand Gulch, Cedar Mesa, Canyonlands, Moab, Arches, Capitol Reef, and the San Rafael Swell. They took more than 2,500 photos and hundreds of pages of field notes. Then they culled their list of favourite hikes down to 95 trips—each selected for its power to incite awe. Their 480-page book describes where to find the redrock cliffs, slickrock domes, soaring arches, and ancient ruins that make southern Utah unique in all the world. And it does so in refreshing style: honest, literate, entertaining, inspiring. Like all *WOW Guides*, this one is full colour throughout, with 220 photos and a trail map for each dayhike and backpack trip. First edition May 2008.

Done in a Day: Whistler
The 10 Premier Hikes

ISBN 978-0-9735099-7-7 Where to invest your limited hiking time to enjoy the greatest scenic reward. Choose an easy, vigourous, or challenging hike. Start your adventure within a short drive of the village. Witness the wonder of Whistler, British Columbia, and be back for a hot shower, great meal, and soft bed. 144 pages, 80 photos, trail maps for each trip, full colour throughout. First edition December 2007.

Done in a Day: Banff
The 10 Premier Hikes

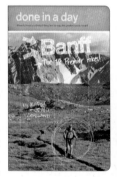

ISBN 978-0-9783427-0-8 Where to invest your limited hiking time to enjoy the greatest scenic reward. Choose an easy, vigourous, or challenging hike. Start your adventure within a short drive of town. Witness the wonder of Banff National Park and be back for a hot shower, great meal, and soft bed. 136 pages, 90 photos, trail maps for each trip, full colour throughout. First edition December 2007.

Done in a Day: Moab
The 10 Premier Hikes

ISBN 978-0-9735099-8-4 Where to invest your limited hiking time to enjoy the greatest scenic reward. Witness the wonder of canyon country — including Arches and Canyonlands national parks — and be back for a hot shower, great meal, and soft bed. 160 pages, 110 photos, trail maps for each trip, full colour. February 2008.

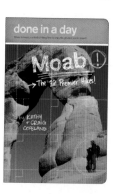

Done in a Day: Calgary
The 10 Premier Road Rides

ISBN 978-0-9783427-3-9 Where to invest your limited cycling time to enjoy the greatest scenic reward. Spring through fall, southwest Alberta offers cyclists blue-ribbon road riding: from alpine passes in the Canadian Rockies, to dinosaur-country river canyons on the edge of the prairie. And this jersey-pocket-sized book is your guide to the ten most serene, compelling, bike-friendly roads in the region. 120 pages, 80 photos, road maps for each ride, full colour. December 2007.

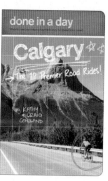

Bears Beware!
How to Avoid an Encounter

The 30-minute MP3 that could save your life. Download it at hikingcamping.com (>Guidebooks >Hiking >Rockies). In bear country, ignorance = risk. Learn simple, specific strategies for safer hiking, especially how to use your voice on the trail to warn away bears. Endorsed by the wardens at Jasper and Waterton national parks.